Dominique's Tropical LATITUDES

Dominique's Tropical LATITUDES

DOMINIQUE MACQUET & JOHN DeMERS

FOOD PHOTOGRAPHY BY SARA ESSEX

BRIGHT SKY PRESS

BRIGHT SKY PRESS

Box 416
Albany, Texas 76430

10   9   8   7   6   5   4   3   2   1

Library of Congress Cataloging-in-Publication Data

Macquet, Dominique.
      Dominique's tropical latitudes / by Dominique Macquet and John DeMers.
           p. cm.
      Includes index.
         ISBN 978-1-933979-01-4 (jacketed hardcover : alk. paper) 1. Cookery, Tropical. 2.
Cookery, International. I. DeMers, John, 1952– II. Title.

TX725.T69M33 2007
641.59—dc22

                                                                                  2007007737

Tropical location photography by John DeMers
Book and cover design by Isabel Lasater Hernandez
Edited by Kristine Krueger
Printed in China through Asia Pacific Offset

Dedication

This book is dedicated to my mother, Marie-Josee Macquet, who taught me first about the wonderful aromas and flavors of the tropical kitchen. Creating these recipes has been as much about remembering her cooking on our melting pot island of Mauritius as about creating something new in the melting pot of New Orleans.

Contents

An Invitation to the Tropics   9

 First Flavors   12

 Signature Soups   32

 Tantalizing Seafood   50

 Meat of the Matter   72

 Sensational Sides   100

 A Rainbow of Desserts   110

 Tropical Drinks   130

 Back to the Basics   138

Tropical Ingredients—Dominique's Glossary   150

Acknowledgments   157

Recipe Index   158

An Invitation to the Tropics

From Chef Dominique Macquet

You *can* go home again. And perhaps, if you're true to yourself, you might never have left it entirely. That has been my story, culinarily and personally, making the long trek across the decades from Mauritius in the Indian Ocean to New Orleans on the Gulf of Mexico. From people older and wiser than me, I gather I'm not the first in human history to drive for what seems like hours and realize I'm just around the corner from the place I began.

Growing up on a tropical island, I relished the "melting pot" into which I was born. Despite historical ties to both France and England, my Mauritius on most days was more about geographic proximity to the exotic, unknowable continent of Africa, where I would someday seek and find my earliest training as a professional chef. It was also more about centuries of immigration, not only from southern Africa but from the mysterious East. Savvy merchants from China and India formed a dazzling background to the French-African culture I knew as "Creole," a culture with its own tangled but delicious cuisine, its own multilayered skin tones and facial appearances, even its own language known as "patois."

When the people of Mauritius wished to speak to those from the outside, we could do so in perfect French or English. When we spoke our own patois, we closed out the rest and had our little world to ourselves. This was an opening and closing I would encounter later, in fascinating ways, in my travels through the Caribbean. It was also something I would find alive and well in my second home, New Orleans.

True to my time and place, the biggest thing I wanted to do with the richness of my native culture was to leave it far behind. My family remained in Mauritius, as families often do, but my eyes were set on the globe-trotting life of a chef. For me, that meant training in South Africa, where I was lucky enough to cook the first meal Nelson Mandela enjoyed after his release from prison; but it also meant an eye-opening apprenticeship in Europe and far, far beyond.

It has been said French was once the "diplomatic language" ... well, among chefs, it remains the culinary one. With classical French training, I felt myself moving, happily and proudly, away from the humble tastes and textures of my tropical childhood. Why sit on a beach and eat a mango, when I can be devouring foie gras flamed in Sauternes? And why eat rustic beans and rice, or spiny lobster in an Indian curry sauce, when sautéed skate wings in caviar cream could be my lot in life? Those were the questions I was asking in those first adventures as a chef. It would be years before I surprised myself with the answers I found in my heart.

The road outward from the Continent began for me, as have many people's roads, in London. While English food can be as tradition-laden as French, London itself proved a huge, cosmopolitan epiphany. It was, in a gargantuan way, what Mauritius had been in a tiny way: a polyglot culture created from the joys and sorrows of colonialism. The sun may have set on the grandeur of the British Empire, but pieces of that empire lived on in the aromas and flavors I found while scouring the backstreets of London. The Indian food alone was worth the trip, pointing me forward in unexpected ways while keeping me ever-grounded in the flavors of my past. Being in London taught me to appreciate the contributions of immigrants everywhere, for I was now an immigrant myself.

And finally, after years of working in a Europe being reborn after union, and after culinary journeys through places as distant as Southeast Asia, my gaze settled eventually on where it *had* to end up all along—the United States. No place in history, I believe, is as boundless in its energy to create, its openness to innovation, its embrace of risk and its delight in triumph as this still-young nation full of people yearning to experience something new.

I'll admit with a smile that cooking in Beverly Hills might not have been the most "normal" of American immigrant experiences, yet much of what I discovered about life and myself there has been true on every American street corner ever since. I was fortunate to find success and acclaim in Beverly Hills, enough to attract the attention of someone looking to bring a new chef to the old city of New Orleans.

I wish I could tell you I understood in minutes why New Orleans felt like home. Perhaps had I been a scholar rather than a chef, I would have. Still, it took me years to find places in my head and heart for the attributes of this strange, exotic and seductive place. I realized quickly, for instance, that many New Orleanians consider themselves "Creoles," and that the authentic food here is called "Creole cuisine." Yet how could I have missed that New Orleans was a tropical colonial city of ancient languages and even more ancient secrets, tied forever to those bright and dark moments that gave us legacies of culture and grace, cruelty, poverty and death? That New Orleans was, in other words, far closer to Mauritius than I could ever realize at the time.

That realization would wait for another day, a day in mid-career when I understood I needed to do something new. Having put my restaurant, Dominique's at the Maison Dupuy Hotel, on the culinary map; having recorded its French-dominated cuisine in a well-received book titled *Dominique's Fresh Flavors: Cooking With Latitude in New Orleans;* having earned enough awards and accolades to last a lifetime, I discovered one day with a shock that I had grown static. I had stopped trying and learning new things in my kitchen. My life was moving forward like a train on which I'd purchased a ticket, yet the doors seemed locked each time we pulled into an interesting station. I wanted something else. No, let me change that: I *needed* something else.

In my quiet moments, when I had them—after the cooks and busboys and dishwashers had all gone home, and I was sipping a Red Stripe beer from Jamaica in my darkened dining room—I slowly tasted in my head new things I might want to cook someday. These things were not French exactly, though some borrowed on the glories of French technique. They were not New Orleans exactly, though the openness and surprise of eating in this Creole city pushed me ever onward. What they were was ... *tropical,* born of a thousand political, social and entrepreneurial dreams on hundreds of outposts beneath palm trees and within a conch shell's throw of white sand and blue water.

You'd need to have lived my life to taste food like this, every stop along the train line. And you'd have to—I realized with a shiver of intense recognition—have embraced your earliest memories on an island 5,000 miles away. I was thinking now, I was dreaming, I was writing down ideas and pieces of recipes ... and before long, I was in the kitchen cooking.

For once in this life of globe-trotting, of seeking and discovering, for once in this life of the exotic and unknown, I knew exactly where I was. I was home.

First Flavors

all them "appetizers" as in the United States or "starters" as in Great Britain or by any other name, the first flavors we touch to our lips in a meal have extraordinary importance. Most chefs understand that these smaller servings often set a tone that continues all evening, whether it's familiar to the point of tedium or fresh, exciting and bracingly new. Obviously, we hope the appetizers that follow strike you as the latter rather than the former.

In addition, it's a truth of the restaurant business that diners order more creative and unusual appetizers than entrées, presumably showing a willingness to gamble more readily with a small beginning than with the entrée they're counting on to fill them up. A marvelous freedom comes with this willingness, as we hope you'll appreciate in the great starter recipes that lie ahead.

Salmon-Crabmeat Roses with Horseradish Crème Fraîche

Salmon-Crabmeat Roses with Horseradi

2 tubs (7 ounces *each*) Dominique's Fleur de Sel

Zest of 10 limes

4 cups sugar

1 side (2 to 3 pounds) fresh salmon, skin on

1 pound fresh horseradish root

2 cups crème fraîche

Salt and black pepper to taste

1 pound lump crabmeat

2 cups diced fresh hearts of palm

Several dishes in this book rely on and showcase the wonderful Fleur de Sel I import into this country from my faraway birthplace on the Indian Ocean island of Mauritius. This favorite reminds us that salt has traditional uses beyond flavor—it was invaluable in the food preservation technique known as curing. In this recipe, salmon is cured before it's wrapped around a mixture of lump crabmeat and hearts of palm.

Combine the fleur de sel, lime zest and sugar; spread across the flesh side of the salmon. Wrap in plastic; turn skin side up and press with weights in the refrigerator for 8 hours.

In a mixing bowl, combine the horseradish root and crème fraîche; season with salt and pepper. Set aside. In another bowl, gently blend the crab and hearts of palm. Brush salt mixture off the salmon; cut salmon into thin slices. Make a "rose" by wrapping three slices of salmon around golf ball-sized balls of crab mixture. Drizzle with horseradish crème fraîche.

Serves 8

Caribbean Conch Ceviche

Caribbean Conch Ceviche

The amazingly tender baby conch I have flown in from the Turks and Caicos Islands are such a change from what people think of as tough or rubbery meat. It's perfect in the starring role in this bright, light ceviche with a twist of tamarind and ginger.

Peel and clean the conch and trim away any rubbery parts; cut into thin matchsticks. Place in a large bowl. Cut the papaya into thin matchsticks and add to the conch. Squeeze lime juice over the top. Purée the dressing ingredients; toss with conch mixture. Chill. Serve in a conch shell with fried plantain chips for garnish.

Serves 10

5 Caribbean farm-raised baby conch, out of shell
1 green papaya
2 limes

Tamarind-Ginger Dressing
¼ cup Tamarind Purée (recipe on page 146)
¼ cup grapeseed oil
¼ cup cold water
1 piece fresh ginger, peeled
¼ jalapeño pepper, seeded
2 teaspoons chopped fresh cilantro
1 teaspoon fresh mint leaves
1 clove garlic

Culinary Origins
23° 7' N – 10° 38' N
82° 21' W – 61° 31' W

Haitian Conch Salad

Haitian Conch Salad

Long known in French as Saint-Domingue, Haiti is one of the most exotic of all islands, and one with profound ties to New Orleans. The slave rebellions of the late 1700s sent refugees black and white into the Crescent City— doubling the population, no less, and bringing a host of intriguing flavors, rhythms and religious practices. This salad is a tribute to those profound links.

10 pieces baby conch, cut into small pieces
4 tomatoes, chopped
1 yellow onion, chopped
½ English cucumber, seeded and cubed
½ Scotch bonnet pepper, seeded and finely chopped
Juice of 1 lime
Juice of 1 lemon
3 teaspoons freshly cracked black pepper
1 teaspoon Dominique's Fleur de Sel

In a mixing bowl, combine all ingredients. Let stand for 10 minutes before serving.

Serves 4

Culinary Origins
18° 33' N
72° 20' W

Surf and Turf Ceviche

Surf and Turf Ceviche

OK, so I'm having fun here. Nothing could seem more boring than a traditional middle-America surf and turf, a way to hustle steak and lobster onto the same plate for diners who can't quite decide. By using the same raw beef we find in steak tartare (but sliced paper-thin like the carpaccio invented at Harry's Bar in Venice) along with salty raw oysters, we turn a cliché on its ear ... or, more precisely, on its shell.

1 pound beef tenderloin
2 pounds fresh horseradish root
Juice of 10 limes
Dominique's Fleur de Sel
Freshly cracked black pepper
24 oysters in shell
½ cup diced Pickled Green Mango (recipe on page 142)

Freeze beef for 5 hours or until firm. Juice the horseradish root in a juicer; place juice in a bowl. Add lime juice, fleur de sel and pepper. Remove oysters from shells, reserving the shells. Place oysters in a bowl and pour juice mixture over the top.

Cut beef into 24 paper-thin slices; lay slices flat. Top each with some pickled mango and one oyster; wrap beef around oyster. Place some pickled mango on each oyster shell; pour a little of the horseradish-lime juice over mango and top with a beef wrap. Sprinkle with pepper and fleur de sel.

Serves 4

Spicy Crawfish atop Fried Green Tomatoes

Spicy Crawfish atop Fried Green Tomatoe

In this recipe, two popular streams join like the tributaries that give New Orleans its Mississippi River. For years, I have served a shrimp dish with this wonderful peppy aioli. Meanwhile, New Orleans-born chefs have not only perfected their own version of remoulade, but have learned to love serving it over that Alabama-Mississippi country classic—fried green tomatoes. It seemed high time for these two streams to flow together.

In a sauté pan over medium heat, sauté the leek leaves in butter until golden. Add red pepper and crawfish tails; sauté for 8 minutes or until liquid evaporates. Stir in chili powder. Remove from the heat; chill.

In a food processor or blender, combine the celery, pickle, onion, celery salt, paprika, garlic, mayonnaise, egg yolk and lemon juice. With the motor running, slowly add peanut oil until fully incorporated. Fold into crawfish mixture; set aside.

Season the green tomato slices with salt and pepper; lightly dust with cornmeal. Preheat oil to 350°. Fry tomatoes until golden, carefully turning once. Drain on paper towels. Serve crawfish mixture over fried tomatoes. Garnish with basil sprigs.

Serves 8

Culinary Origins
29° 53' N
91° 54' W

¼ cup diced green leek leaves

1 tablespoon unsalted butter

1 red bell pepper, chopped

1 pound crawfish tails, peeled and cooked, with liquid

1 teaspoon chili powder

2 ribs celery, diced

1 large dill pickle, diced

1 medium red onion, sliced

½ tablespoon celery salt

1 teaspoon paprika

1 teaspoon chopped garlic

3 tablespoons Homemade Mayonnaise (recipe on page 147)

1 egg yolk

1 tablespoon fresh lemon juice

1 cup peanut oil

Fried Green Tomatoes

4 green tomatoes, sliced ½ inch thick

Salt and freshly ground black pepper

½ cup cornmeal

¼ cup vegetable *or* peanut oil

Basil sprigs for garnish

Phyllo-Goat Cheese Purses
with Onion Fricassee

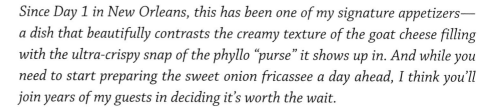

10 white onions, chopped

2 cups balsamic vinegar, *divided*

1 cup honey, *divided*

2 teaspoons chopped fresh thyme

1 package (16 ounces) frozen phyllo
   dough, thawed

¼ cup clarified butter

11 ounces goat cheese

Mâche lettuce for garnish

Since Day 1 in New Orleans, this has been one of my signature appetizers—a dish that beautifully contrasts the creamy texture of the goat cheese filling with the ultra-crispy snap of the phyllo "purse" it shows up in. And while you need to start preparing the sweet onion fricassee a day ahead, I think you'll join years of my guests in deciding it's worth the wait.

To make the fricassee, in a large saucepan over low heat, cook the onions for 4 hours in their natural juices. Refrigerate overnight.

The next day, cook the onions for another 2 hours over medium heat until they reach the consistency of jam. Add 1 cup vinegar and ½ cup honey; reduce over medium heat until dry, stirring often, about 2 hours (mixture should have a thick consistency). Cool. Stir in thyme.

Preheat oven to 300°. Layer four sheets of phyllo dough, brushing butter between each layer. Cut dough in half and repeat three times (each stack of four sheets makes two portions). Divide the goat cheese into six equal portions. Place a piece of cheese in the middle of dough; add a tablespoon of fricassee. Wrap phyllo around filling, gathering at the top and twisting to secure (like a beggar's purse). Place on a baking sheet. Bake for 5–6 minutes.

Combine the remaining vinegar and honey; drizzle over purses. Garnish with mâche lettuce.

Serves 6

Culinary Origins
43° 31′ N
5° 27′ E

Curried Lamb and Chickpea Samosas

Almost every great food culture on Earth has a dish like this ... people seem to like seasoned meat in a flaky pastry crust wherever you happen to visit or live. Here's an Indian-flavored variation, although the differently seasoned empanadas of Hispanic America can be terrific, too. Of course, you can make your own pastry from scratch, but I think most people will prefer to concentrate on the filling and use one of the fine phyllo dough products on sale in supermarkets today.

Heat oil in a large pan; sauté the lamb until browned. Add onions and garlic; cook and stir until caramelized. Add the chickpeas and garam masala; stir for 3–5 minutes. Drain through a fine sieve for 15–20 minutes. Sprinkle with cilantro. Cool.

Preheat oven to 350°. Unfold the phyllo (as you're working, keep dough covered with a damp cloth so it doesn't dry out). Cut dough into 5-inch squares. Layer three squares of dough in a stack; spoon about 1 tablespoon of lamb mixture onto bottom corner. Fold dough over the top diagonally to form a triangle; seal edges with melted butter. Repeat with remaining dough, filling and butter. Place the triangles on a lightly greased baking sheet. Bake for 10 minutes or until golden.

Serves 8

1 tablespoon olive oil

1 pound ground lamb

2 medium onions, chopped

3 cloves garlic, minced

1 cup cooked chickpeas

2 tablespoons Homemade Garam Masala (recipe on page 140)

2 tablespoons chopped fresh cilantro

1 package (16 ounces) frozen phyllo dough, thawed

½ cup butter, melted

Culinary Origins
18° 56′ N
72° 51′ E

Ahi Tuna and Crispy Pineapple

Ahi Tuna and Crispy Pineapple

Pineapple Mille-Feuille

1 fresh pineapple, peeled
1 tablespoon grapeseed oil

Soy-Ginger Vinaigrette

¼ cup soy sauce
¼ cup grapeseed oil
2 tablespoons sesame oil
2 tablespoons fresh lime juice
2 tablespoons minced fresh ginger
2 tablespoons diced shallots
1 tablespoon chopped garlic

2 cups diced sushi-grade tuna
½ cup diced green bell pepper
½ cup diced red bell pepper
¼ cup diced red onion
1 cucumber, thinly sliced

For sheer delicacy, but with a lot of flavor, it's hard to beat this popular starter from my restaurant. Sushi lovers, of course, immediately zero in on the tuna and the soy-ginger vinaigrette. But lovers of the tropics respond at least as much to the wispy-crispy slices of sweet oven-dried pineapple.

Preheat oven to 200°. Slice the pineapple into paper-thin slices and arrange on a baking sheet; brush lightly with oil. Bake for 4 hours until crispy like a potato chip.

In a stainless steel mixing bowl, combine the vinaigrette ingredients. Cover and chill for 1 hour.

In another stainless steel mixing bowl, combine the tuna, bell peppers, onion and ½ cup vinaigrette. On each plate, arrange thin slices of cucumber in a circle, with slices slightly overlapping. Place a ring mold in center of plate; fill with a pineapple chip and a layer of tuna mixture. Repeat layers, ending with a pineapple chip. Drizzle remaining vinaigrette around plate surface. Remove ring mold and serve.

Serves 4

Pompano Tartare

With the popularity of sushi in this country, all chefs have been liberated from what seems a tradition of cooking fish into submission. In other words, diners don't mind if fish is still fresh and juicy and wonderful—the way it should be—rather than dried out and tasting like cardboard. Even dishes like this seafood spin on steak tartare find a ready audience. And who wouldn't enjoy a side order of malanga chips?

½ Pickled Lemon (recipe on page 143), finely diced,
    with 2 tablespoons juice
1 tablespoon ginger juice
1 cup extra virgin olive oil
1 tablespoon Dominique's Fleur de Sel
1 teaspoon cracked black pepper
1 whole bulb fennel
1 whole pompano (2 pounds), cut into small cubes
2 whole malanga, sliced very thin and fried until crisp

For vinaigrette, in a mixing bowl, combine the pickled lemon with both juices; whisk in oil. Lightly season with fleur de sel and pepper. Using a mandoline, slice fennel very thin; mix with a little of the vinaigrette. Combine the pompano with the remaining vinaigrette. Fill a ring mold halfway with pompano; add shaved fennel. Sprinkle with fleur de sel and pepper. Garnish with malanga chips.

Serves 4

Grilled Lollipop Wings with Peri-Peri

Peri-peri is a hot sauce favored in Africa and a flavor I love. Bottled in Africa, it may be available in stores that have a big collection of opportunities to burn your mouth. Still, here's a terrific recipe for making your own. If you think of these (to seriously mix metaphors and geographies) as African Buffalo Wings, you'll get some idea of the appeal. Making the wings into "lollipops" is just for visual fun.

To make the peri-peri sauce, sauté onions and garlic in ¼ cup oil over medium heat for 4 minutes. Cool. Place the lemons, hot peppers, seasonings, onion mixture and remaining oil in a food processor; cover and purée.

With a paring knife, cut drumettes on one side and pull the skin down; remove any skin by scraping with knife. Pull meat down to form a ball at one end, leaving bone clean like a lollipop stick. Set aside 1 cup peri-peri sauce for basting. Pour the remaining sauce into a baking pan; add wings. Cover and refrigerate overnight.

Preheat oven to 300°. Bake wings for 10 minutes. Remove from pan and discard marinade. Grill wings for 10 minutes, brushing with reserved sauce. Serve with Sauce Raita.

Serves 4

3 yellow onions, chopped

1 tablespoon minced garlic

3 cups pomace olive oil, *divided*

2 Pickled Lemons
(recipe on page 143)

3 cayenne *or* Asian hot peppers, seeded

1 cup ground chimayo pepper

1 tablespoon ground cumin

1 tablespoon ground coriander

½ teaspoon freshly ground black pepper

½ teaspoon sea salt

24 chicken wing drumettes, small wing removed

Sauce Raita (recipe on page 145)

Culinary Origins
29° 53' S
31° 0' E

Shrimp and Foie Gras Ravioli with Leek Fondue

Shrimp and Foie Gras Ravioli with Leek

Diners in my restaurant have embraced my personal take on one of Italy's most popular pasta shapes. I think you'll love the filling of shrimp and foie gras, not to mention the frothy sauce. Be sure you don't make the sauce until the very end, since those luscious bubbles just don't keep.

Pasta Dough
2 cups high-gluten flour
1 teaspoon salt
²/₃ cup water

Filling
8 medium shrimp, peeled and deveined
3 ounces foie gras, cleaned
Salt and black pepper to taste
1 egg beaten with 2 tablespoons water

Fondue
1 cup julienned leek (white portion only)
3 tablespoons unsalted butter
4 pieces (1 ounce *each*) foie gras
4 large shrimp, peeled and deveined

Sauce
2 cups Shrimp Stock (recipe on page 149)
2 cups Duck Stock (recipe on page 148)
1 ounce foie gras, diced

In the bowl of a stand mixer, combine flour and salt; using the dough hook attachment, mix on low speed. Add water gradually. Turn off mixer and scrape dough onto a dry, lightly floured countertop. Knead until smooth, about 10 minutes; cover with plastic wrap and let rest in the refrigerator for 1 hour.

For filling, purée shrimp in a blender until smooth. Add foie gras; purée until incorporated. Season with salt and pepper. Divide rested dough in half; feed through a pasta maker, starting at the thickest setting and working down to 1.5. Cut dough into 3¹/₂-inch rounds. Divide filling equally over four rounds. Brush edges with egg wash; top with remaining rounds and press edges to seal.

Cook the leek slowly in butter for 15 minutes; drain and keep warm. In a sauté pan, sear the foie gras pieces; remove. In the same pan, sauté shrimp for 3–4 minutes. For sauce, reduce stocks by one-third; mix in diced foie gras with a hand blender until frothy. Meanwhile, cook ravioli in salted water for 3–4 minutes.

Place one piece of ravioli in each bowl; add a piece of seared foie gras, one sautéed shrimp and some leek fondue. Spoon frothy sauce around ravioli.

Serves 4

Foie Gras on Fried Plantain Rounds

Foie Gras on Fried Plantain Rounds

1 whole foie gras (1 to 1½ pounds)

4 ripe plantains, peeled

½ cup dark rum

1 cup fresh pineapple juice

3 cups Duck Stock
   (recipe on page 148)

Dominique's Fleur de Sel

Plantains, as you may know, are solid and starchy before they get ripe, then embark on a slow sweetening as they ripen to come out close to bananas. For this dish, we definitely want some sweetness, so be sure to use ripe plantains. There are many traditions of pairing foie gras with fruit (or with fruit-intense dessert wines like Sauternes). In this one, we take that idea to the tropics.

Preheat oven to 400°. In a sauté pan over high heat, sear the foie gras on all sides until golden brown. Transfer to another pan; place in the oven.

Slice plantains on a bias into 2½-inch-thick rounds. Using a cleaver, smash each round until 1 inch flat. Sauté in the foie gras fat until golden brown on both sides. Place eight rounds on a baking sheet; place in the oven. Chop the remaining rounds and return to the pan with the foie gras fat.

Remove foie gras from the oven; pour pan drippings over the chopped plantains. Add rum and pineapple juice; cook for 4 minutes or until liquor has evaporated. Add stock; reduce by one-third. Purée this mixture in a blender.

Set crispy plantain rounds on a small plate; top with a slice of foie gras and drizzle with the reduced sauce. Sprinkle with fleur de sel.

Serves 8

Culinary Origins
23° 7' N
82° 21' W

Meat Patties

To make the pastry, sift together the flour, 1½ teaspoons garam masala and salt; cut in shortening until the mixture looks like peas. Add just enough ice water to hold the dough together. Wrap in plastic wrap and refrigerate for at least 12 hours.

To make the filling, combine the beef, lamb, onions and Scotch bonnet. Heat oil in a skillet; brown the meat mixture for 10 minutes. Stir in the bread crumbs, thyme, salt, pepper and remaining garam masala. Add ½ cup water; cover and simmer for 30 minutes. Cool to room temperature.

Remove pastry from the refrigerator and let stand for 15 minutes. On a lightly floured surface, roll out to ¼-inch thickness; cut into 4-inch circles. Sprinkle a little flour on each circle and stack; cover with a damp towel.

Preheat oven to 400°. Divide the filling evenly over half of each circle; fold plain half of pastry over filling and seal edges with a fork. Place on baking sheets. Bake for 30 minutes or until golden brown.

Makes 1 dozen

2 cups all-purpose flour

2½ teaspoons Homemade Garam Masala (recipe on page 140), *divided*

½ teaspoon salt

½ cup vegetable shortening

Ice water

½ pound ground beef

¼ ground ground lamb

1 yellow onion, diced

2 green onions, thinly sliced

1 Scotch bonnet pepper, seeded and finely chopped

3 tablespoons olive oil

¾ cup unseasoned bread crumbs

½ teaspoon dried thyme

Salt and freshly ground black pepper to taste

Patties is the Jamaican name given to these meat pies, yet the "curry" flavors in the filling and even in the pastry testify to the strong influence of the Caribbean's immigrants from India. As with the English themselves (chicken tikka masala is now called "England's national dish"), generations of Jamaicans have loved and lived on their beloved patties.

Peri-Peri Grilled Shrimp Caesar Salad

Peri-Peri Grilled Shrimp Caesar Salad

12 large shrimp, peeled

1 cup Peri-Peri Sauce
(recipe on page 141)

3 tablespoons olive oil

½ loaf rustic Italian bread, cut into
1-inch cubes

1 teaspoon Dominique's Fleur de Sel

¼ cup Homemade Mayonnaise
(recipe on page 147)

2 teaspoons Worcestershire sauce

½ teaspoon freshly ground black
pepper

1 tablespoon fresh lemon juice

1 tablespoon grated Parmesan cheese

1 large head romaine, roughly chopped

I was brought up in the classical tradition, in which salads were cooling, refreshing intermezzos, preferably between a dinner's seafood and meat course. Still, for a lot of good reasons, many people enjoy salads as their entire lunch and sometimes even as their entire dinner. If I were making an entrée salad for myself, this pungent one with grilled shrimp and African peri-peri hot sauce is what I'd make.

Marinate the shrimp in peri-peri sauce for 30 minutes. Meanwhile, for croutons, heat oil in a sauté pan; fry bread cubes until golden on all sides, about 2–3 minutes. Drain on paper towels; sprinkle with fleur de sel. To make the dressing, combine the mayonnaise, Worcestershire sauce, pepper, lemon juice and Parmesan cheese.

Grill the shrimp just until done, about 2 minutes on each side. Toss romaine with the dressing; divide among four salad bowls. Top with grilled shrimp and croutons. Sprinkle with additional Parmesan and pepper.

Serves 4

Culinary Origins
29° 53' S
31° 0' E

Cool Watercress-Romaine Salad

Cool Watercress-Romaine Salad

For a nice, comfortable, but still very interesting salad, consider the elements of this one. I love the mix of cool romaine and more "peppery" watercress, while the oven-dried tomatoes and crispy roasted corn insert all kinds of neat textures beneath a blanket of citrus and mustard.

Combine the oven-dried tomato ingredients; spread in a single layer on a baking sheet. Place in a 150° oven for 8 hours.

To make the vinaigrette, combine the juices and mustard with a hand blender. Slowly add oil, blending to emulsify. Season with salt and pepper. In a bowl, combine the romaine, watercress and corn; add vinaigrette and toss lightly. Top with oven-dried tomatoes.

Serves 10

Oven-Dried Tomatoes

10 Roma tomatoes, peeled

¼ bunch fresh thyme

8 cloves garlic, minced

1 tablespoon sugar

Salt and freshly ground black pepper

¼ cup olive oil

Citrus-Mustard Vinaigrette

½ cup orange juice

½ cup lemon juice

½ cup lime juice

½ cup grapefruit juice

¼ cup Dijon mustard

1½ cups olive oil

Salt and freshly ground black pepper
  to taste

5 hearts of romaine, broken into leaves

3 bunches baby watercress

1 cup whole kernel corn, roasted

Signature Soups

ho can say enough great things about soup? For starters, as the saying goes, soup truly is good food—an affordable and nutritious source that feeds people the world over, whether as part of a meal or the meal itself. Beyond that, soup is a no-holds-barred delivery system than runs on broth or no broth, cream or no cream, and any conceivable combination of meat, seafood or vegetables.

It's hard to think of any cuisine on Earth that lacks a signature soup, or that fails to rely on soup to deliver health and comfort in high times and low. We tour the soup globe in this chapter, from a new-and-improved version of Caribbean conch chowder to a spin on Vietnamese beef pho with a spoonful of fusion pesto on top.

Lastly, it can be no accident that what might be the world's most popular food is also the easiest to make. Sure, we chefs can give you lots of extra hoops to jump through in pursuit of sublime flavor, but we should never forget what a simple and direct proposition the making of soup really is.

Crawfish and Watercress Soup

Crawfish and Watercress Soup

½ cup finely chopped onion

2 cloves garlic, minced

2 tablespoons olive oil

2 potatoes, peeled and chopped

1 tablespoon chopped fresh thyme

1 pound fresh watercress, washed,
  stemmed and chopped

6 cups Crawfish Stock
  (recipe on page 148)

6 cups Chicken Stock
  (recipe on page 148)

20 crawfish tails, peeled and cooked

Saffron Oyster Toasts

1 cup Chicken Stock
  (recipe on page 148)

¼ teaspoon saffron threads

8 fresh oysters

1 egg, beaten

1 cup grated Gruyère cheese

8 slices French bread

While taste is certainly important in a soup, or any other dish, I've always been equally fascinated by texture. The old French chefs didn't invent croutons for nothing! That's the texture idea behind the Saffron Oyster Toasts, but the taste carries us far beyond crispy squares of French bread.

In a soup pot, sauté onion and garlic in oil for 3 minutes. Add potatoes; cook 3 minutes longer. Add thyme and watercress. Stir in the stocks. Bring to a rolling boil. Remove from the heat; purée in a blender. Return to the pot. Add crawfish; heat through. Keep warm.

Preheat oven to 350°. In a saucepan, bring stock and saffron to a boil. Add oysters; remove from the heat and poach for 1 minute. Remove oysters from stock; when cool enough to handle, cut in half. Combine oyster halves with egg and cheese; spoon onto bread slices. Place on a baking sheet. Bake for 5 minutes or until golden brown.

Ladle soup into four bowls; top each with two oyster toasts.

Serves 4

Culinary Origins
29° 57' N
90° 4' W

Shrimp and Artichoke Soup

Shrimp and Artichoke Soup

Shrimp and artichokes are two favorite ingredients around New Orleans, though not used together as often as I'd like. In this soup, shrimp is not only the flavor in the stock but, once grilled and diced, the garnish as well.

In a soup pot, heat oil over medium heat; sauté artichoke bottoms for 2 minutes. Add shallots, garlic, carrots and celery; cook for 5 minutes or until lightly caramelized. Add stock. Bring to a quick boil, about 2 minutes. Add spinach.

   Remove from the heat. Purée in a blender until smooth; strain through chinois. Season with salt and pepper. Ladle into soup bowls; garnish with shrimp.

Serves 6

¼ cup vegetable oil

3 large raw artichoke bottoms, roughly chopped

¼ cup chopped shallots

1 tablespoon chopped garlic

¼ cup chopped carrots

¼ cup chopped celery

6 cups Shrimp Stock (recipe on page 149)

½ cup fresh spinach leaves

Salt and black pepper to taste

12 small shrimp, grilled and diced

Culinary Origins
29° 57' N
90° 4' W

Mulligatawny Soup

Mulligatawny Soup

½ cup plus 2 tablespoons chopped
   fresh parsley, *divided*

3 tablespoons minced garlic, *divided*

10 fresh basil leaves

1 stem lemongrass, cut lengthwise

1 tablespoon grated ginger

1 teaspoon crushed red pepper

1 chicken (2 to 3 pounds), cut into
   pieces

15 cups Chicken Stock
   (recipe on page 148), *divided*

1 fresh coconut

1 tablespoon Tamarind Purée
   (recipe on page 146)

3 tablespoons vegetable oil

2 yellow onions, finely chopped

8 tomatoes, blanched, peeled and
   diced

2 jalapeño peppers, seeded and
   chopped

2 tablespoons finely chopped ginger

3 tablespoons Homemade Curry
   Powder (recipe on page 140)

1 teaspoon Homemade Garam
   Masala (recipe on page 140)

1 teaspoon finely chopped fresh
   thyme

Salt and black pepper to taste

Steamed basmati rice

There's no question where this recipe comes from—my mother's kitchen on the isle of Mauritius when I was little—a fact that makes the taste memory very special. The concept is Indian through and through, but most scholars believe the name "Mulligatawny" was actually a British invention. Makes sense to me, since the British love their curry almost as much as I do.

Combine ½ cup parsley, 1 tablespoon garlic, basil, lemongrass, grated ginger and red pepper; rub over chicken pieces. Marinate for 30 minutes. Poach chicken in 7 cups stock for 1 hour. Cool. Reserve poaching stock. Shred chicken; discard bones.

Cut coconut and reserve juice; grate coconut meat and mix into juice. Add tamarind; mix well. Strain through chinois and reserve liquid.

In a soup pot, heat oil over medium heat. Sauté onions and remaining garlic until soft, about 2 minutes. Add tomatoes, jalapeños and chopped ginger; cook for 5 minutes. Add curry powder, garam masala and thyme; cook for 3 minutes.

Add remaining stock and reserved poaching stock. Bring to a boil. Stir in shredded chicken and reserved coconut-tamarind liquid. Season with salt and pepper. Simmer for 5 minutes. Spoon basmati rice into the center of soup bowls; ladle soup around rice. Garnish with remaining parsley.

Serves 6–8

Culinary Origins
18° 56' N
72° 51' E

Coconut Crab Soup

Coconut Crab Soup

Diners in my restaurant always leave talking about this striking Asian soup—probably more Thai than anything else—with its lemongrass and coconut milk. The only trick is using a juicer to extract the ginger, cilantro, jalapeño and garlic juices, but I think the payoff in the bowl is worth the effort.

8 cups Crab Stock (recipe on page 148)
2 cups Coconut Milk (recipe on page 147)
½ cup light soy sauce
2 tablespoons ginger juice
2 tablespoons cilantro juice
1 tablespoon jalapeño juice
½ tablespoon garlic juice
2 tablespoons chopped lemongrass (tender insides only)
1 cup lump crabmeat
Chopped fresh cilantro

In a soup pot, heat stock over high heat. Add milk. Bring to a boil. Add soy sauce, juices and lemongrass. Remove from the heat. Ladle into soup bowls; garnish with crab and cilantro.

Serves 6–8

Culinary Origins
13° 44′ N
100° 30′ E

Conch and White Bean Chowder

Conch and White Bean Chowder

2 cups dried white beans

5 cups water

1 pound bacon, sliced

½ cup finely chopped shallots, *divided*

½ cup finely chopped celery, *divided*

¼ cup finely chopped leeks (white portion only)

6 cups Chicken Stock (recipe on page 148)

1 piece ham hock

10 farm-raised baby conch, pounded flat and finely chopped

6 cups Lobster Stock (recipe on page 149)

Salt and freshly ground black pepper to taste

Culinary Origins
23° 7' N – 10° 38' N
82° 21' W – 61° 31' W

Bacon provides the flavor and conch provides the protein for this satisfying soup from the islands. I prefer this puréed version, but it tastes equally wonderful with all its components intact.

Soak the beans in water for 1 hour. Meanwhile, in a sauté pan over low heat, render the bacon for 5 minutes. Remove ¼ cup plus 3 tablespoons bacon fat; set aside. Chop the bacon into bits; set aside for garnish. In a stockpot, heat ¼ cup reserved bacon fat; sauté ¼ cup shallots, ¼ cup celery and leeks for 5 minutes.

Add chicken stock and ham hock. Drain beans; add to the pot. Bring to a quick boil over high heat. Reduce heat; simmer for 30 minutes. Check to ensure beans are fully cooked and tender. Remove and discard ham hock. Purée the soup and strain through chinois; set aside.

In a soup pot, heat 3 tablespoons reserved bacon fat; sauté the conch for 4 minutes. Add remaining shallots and celery; sauté 3 minutes longer. Add lobster stock and puréed white bean mixture. Bring to a boil; heat through. Season with salt and pepper. Ladle into soup bowls; garnish with bacon bits.

Serves 6–8

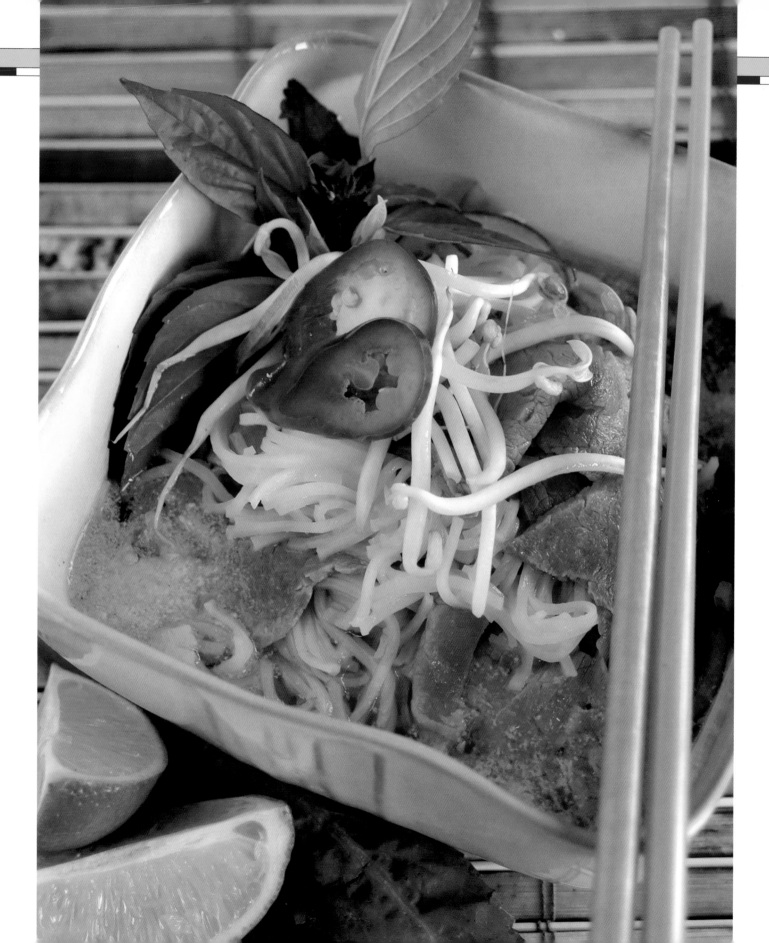

Beef Pho with Ming's Asian Pesto

Beef Pho with Ming's Asian Pesto

As more and more Americans know, pho is the soup people in Vietnam can enjoy for three meals a day. This recipe combines a traditional approach to the savory beef broth and noodles with an East-West pesto I cooked on TV with my friend Ming Tsai. By the way, most scholars think the name "pho" (pronounced more like "fuh") came into use in Vietnam during the French colonial period, when the soup was inspired by the classic "pot au feu."

5 to 6 pounds beef soup bones
1 pound beef chuck *or* brisket, cut into pieces
2 yellow onions, lightly charred over flame
1 piece gingerroot (4 inches), peeled and lightly charred
6 whole cloves
5 whole star anise
1 cinnamon stick (3 inches)
1½ teaspoons salt
4 tablespoons Vietnamese *or* Thai fish sauce
6 quarts water

Asian Pesto
1½ cups roasted peanuts
Whole cloves from 2 heads elephant garlic, roasted
10 leaves green shiso
1 cup Thai basil leaves
¼ cup fresh mint leaves
¼ cup fresh cilantro leaves
4 Serrano peppers
½ cup peanut oil

1 yellow onion, thinly sliced
1½ pounds small dried banh pho noodles (rice sticks)
½ pound round sirloin of London broil
4 scallions (green portion only), chopped
⅓ cup chopped fresh cilantro
Freshly ground black pepper to taste

To make a clear broth, parboil the soup bones and beef in water for 3–5 minutes to release the impurities. Drain and rinse with fresh water, cleaning any residue from the stockpot. Return the bones and meat to the pot. Add the next eight ingredients. Bring to a boil. Reduce heat to a gentle simmer; cook for 3 hours, skimming impurities from the top occasionally.

Meanwhile, in a blender or food processor, purée peanuts and roasted garlic until smooth. Add the shiso, basil, mint, cilantro and peppers. When mixture has became a green paste, slowly add oil with the blender running, incorporating thoroughly. Set aside.

Soak sliced onion in cold water for 30 minutes. Meanwhile, soak the dried noodles in hot tap water for 15–20 minutes or until softened, and freeze the beef for 15 minutes. Cut beef into paper-thin slices. Quickly blanch the noodles in boiling water, just 10–15 seconds; remove with a strainer and divide among eight soup bowls. Top with beef and soaked onion.

Strain the broth and bring just to a boil; ladle into bowls, cooking the beef. Top each bowl with a spoonful of pesto; garnish with scallions, cilantro and pepper.

Serves 8

Oxtail and Pigeon Pea Soup

Oxtail and Pigeon Pea Soup

1 pound dried pigeon peas

5 pounds oxtail, cut into 2½-inch
    pieces

5 ribs celery, finely chopped

2 yellow onions, finely chopped

4 carrots, finely chopped

8 tomatoes, chopped

1 teaspoon chopped fresh thyme

8 cups Chicken Stock
    (recipe on page 148)

Yucca Croutons

2 whole yucca, peeled and cut into
    small cubes

¼ to ½ cup butter

Salt and freshly ground black pepper
    to taste

½ cup chopped fresh parsley

Culinary Origins
18° 30' N
69° 57' W

It doesn't ever get really cold on the islands, but nevertheless, islanders think of something like this oxtail soup whenever the temperature plummets below about 55. Except for the hip Nuevo Latino yucca croutons, this is a very old-fashioned dish, delivering old-fashioned pleasure.

Soak the peas for 3 hours. Meanwhile, preheat oven to 275°. Braise the oxtail in a large pot over medium heat for 5 minutes or until golden brown. Add celery, onions and carrots; caramelize for 5 minutes. Add tomatoes, thyme and stock. Bring to a quick boil. Cover the pot with foil. Place in the oven for 2 hours.

Strain and discard vegetables. Reserve the oxtail. Drain pigeon peas; add to braising liquid. Cook over low heat for 15 minutes; strain. Purée half of the peas in a blender. Shred oxtail meat; combine with puréed peas. Add remaining peas and braising liquid; keep warm.

To make the croutons, blanch the yucca cubes in boiling water for 5 minutes or until fully cooked. Cool; dry on paper towels. In a sauté pan, fry yucca in butter until golden brown. Season with salt and pepper. Ladle soup into soup bowls; garnish with yucca croutons and parsley.

Serves 6

Breadfruit Soup
with Truffles and Foie Gras

Breadfruit Soup with Truffles and Foie

Breadfruit is the potato of the tropical world, used in everything from fried chips to mayonnaise-smooth "potato salad." The plant itself was brought to the Caribbean from tropical Asia by none other than Captain Bligh, the notorious officer who got booted off the Bounty.

In a soup pot over medium heat, cook the stock and breadfruit for 20 minutes or until a knife goes easily through the fruit. Remove from the heat; purée in a blender. In a small saucepan, heat the cream with truffle butter until it starts to reduce; add to the blender and emulsify with the breadfruit mixture.

Return mixture to the soup pot; heat through. Ladle into soup bowls; garnish with truffle slices and diced foie gras.

Serves 8

8 cups Chicken Stock
(recipe on page 148)
1 green breadfruit (2 pounds), peeled
and diced
1 cup heavy cream
2 tablespoons prepared truffle butter
1 whole black truffle, sliced into 16
thin pieces
3 ounces foie gras, deveined and diced

Culinary Origins
18° 29' N
66° 8' W

Mango Soup with Lime Zest

This may be the shortest recipe I've ever written, and possibly the easiest to make. But you'll be amazed how good it is on a hot summer day.

4 mangoes
4 cans (12 ounces *each*) 7Up
Zest of 2 limes
4 fresh mint leaves

Peel mangoes and remove stones; place in a blender. Add the 7Up and lime juice; purée. Refrigerate until chilled. Pour into soup bowls; garnish with mint.

Serves 4

Culinary Origins
21° 18' N
157° 51' W

Red Bean Soup with Spinners

Red Bean Soup with Spinners

In some tropical places, the dumplings that add substance to this soup are colorfully called "spinners." Still, whatever you call them, it's pretty clear that here is a filling and satisfying meal requiring no expensive ingredients ... always a good formula for people who cook for their families every day.

Soak the dried kidney beans overnight. Drain and discard the water; set beans aside. In a soup pot, sauté the salt pork and bacon in oil. Drain, reserving 2 tablespoons fat. Sauté the onion, celery, carrot, garlic and Scotch bonnets until golden. Add the soaked beans, stock, potatoes, green onions and thyme. Simmer until beans are tender, about 1 hour.

    To make the dumplings, combine the flour and salt in a small bowl; add just enough water to create a stiff dough. Pinch 2 tablespoonfuls of dough and shape into long, thin dumplings. Add to simmering soup and cook for 15 minutes. Season with salt and pepper. Ladle into a tureen or soup bowls.

Serves 8

2 pounds dried red kidney beans

½ pound salt pork, cut into strips

2 slices bacon, chopped

1 tablespoon olive oil

1 yellow onion, finely chopped

1 rib celery, finely chopped

1 carrot, finely chopped

1 teaspoon minced garlic

2 Scotch bonnet peppers, seeded
   and chopped

4 quarts Chicken Stock
   (recipe on page 148)

½ pound potatoes, peeled and cubed

3 green onions, chopped

2 sprigs fresh thyme

1 cup all-purpose flour

¼ teaspoon salt

Water

Salt and freshly ground black pepper
   to taste

Culinary Origins
23° 7' N – 10° 38' N
82° 21' W – 61° 31' W

Surprise Coconut Shrimp Soup

Surprise Coconut Shrimp Soup

Smoked Snapper Rillette

1 snapper fillet (½ pound), skin and
   bones removed

1 cup Indian Vindaye
   (recipe on page 142)

4 cups hickory wood chips, *divided*

1 cup water

Soup

1 cup Coconut Milk
   (recipe on page 147)

3 cups Shrimp Stock
   (recipe on page 149)

1 kaffir lime leaf, finely chopped

½ cup light soy sauce

2 tablespoons ginger juice

2 tablespoons cilantro juice

1 tablespoon jalapeño juice

½ tablespoon garlic juice

2 leek leaves

Culinary Origins
23° 7' N – 10° 38' N
82° 21' W – 61° 31' W

This is another of those light, Asian-tinged soups that guests love so much in my restaurant. In the spirit of American breakfast cereals, there's a surprise at the bottom of the bowl.

Place snapper in a shallow pan; pour vindaye on top. Cover with plastic wrap and refrigerate overnight, about 10–15 hours.

Soak 2 cups of wood chips in water. Place remaining chips on the bottom of a grill or smoker; light the chips. When they're burning, add the water-soaked chips to create smoke. Immediately place the snapper above the smoke; cold-smoke for 30–40 minutes. Check every 15 minutes to ensure fire is still burning.

Meanwhile, in a soup pot, bring milk and stock to a boil. Add lime leaf; boil 5 minutes longer. Strain. Stir in the soy sauce and juices; simmer until ready to serve. Blanch leek leaves in boiling water; drain and cool.

When fish is cooked, remove from fire and shred with a small fork. This shredded fish is called "rillette." Cut leek leaves into four pieces; place rillette in center of each leaf. Fold leaf over and wrap into a parcel. Place each parcel in a soup bowl; ladle hot soup on top.

Serves 4

Pepperpot

Each Caribbean island has its own ideas about what pepperpot really is, but it's the single most popular soup in the region. It's as though each population meets every 10 years or so to decide which ingredients must go in and which can never be included, and that is that … at least until you get to the next island!

In a soup pot, sauté salt pork in oil for 10 minutes, rendering the fat. Drain, reserving 2 tablespoons fat. Sauté the pork cubes, onions, garlic and Scotch bonnets until onions are golden, about 5 minutes. Add the remaining ingredients. Cover and simmer for 2 hours. Remove the salt pork before serving. Ladle into soup bowls.

Serves 6–8

¼ pound salt pork, cut into strips

1 tablespoon olive oil

½ pound fresh lean pork, cubed

2 yellow onions, thinly sliced

1 teaspoon minced garlic

2 Scotch bonnet peppers, seeded and chopped

8 cups Chicken Stock (recipe on page 148)

20 pods fresh okra, chopped

2 pounds fresh kale, cleaned and chopped

½ pound fresh callaloo *or* spinach, cleaned and chopped

1 tablespoon chopped fresh thyme

1 teaspoon ground cumin

Freshly ground black pepper to taste

Gazpacho with Creole Mustard Ice Cream
Gazpacho with Creole Mustard Ice Cream

Everybody loves this Spanish specialty—chilled soup usually made with tomato and a host of other vegetables that give each spoonful a bracing crunch. In my gazpacho, all that happens … and more, thanks to the scoop of ice cream in the center with a little kick from Creole mustard.

Place the soup ingredients in a food processor or blender; purée. Refrigerate until chilled.

To make the ice cream, in a large saucepan, bring milk and cream to a boil. In a large bowl, whisk the egg yolks; slowly stir in hot milk mixture. Cool quickly by placing bowl in an ice-water bath. Stir in the mustard. Freeze in an ice cream maker according to the manufacturer's instructions.

Pour gazpacho into soup bowls; place a scoop of ice cream in the middle.

Serves 8

Soup

10 Oven-Dried Tomatoes
(recipe on page 31)
2 cups chopped mixed green, red
and yellow bell peppers
1 cup chopped seeded cucumber
1 small yellow onion, chopped
½ cup chopped celery
3 tablespoons chopped fresh parsley
2 tablespoons extra virgin olive oil
1 tablespoon chopped fresh thyme
1 teaspoon Dominique's Fleur de Sel
1 teaspoon freshly cracked black
pepper

Ice Cream

1 quart whole milk
1 cup heavy cream
10 egg yolks
½ cup coarse-grain Creole mustard

Culinary Origins
22° 18′ N
97° 52′ W

Tantalizing Seafood

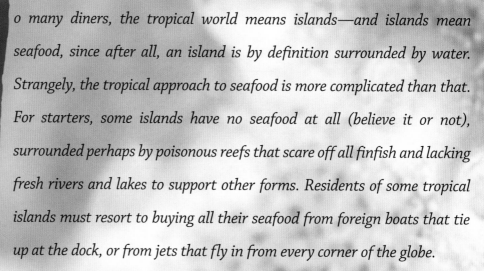

To many diners, the tropical world means islands—and islands mean seafood, since after all, an island is by definition surrounded by water. Strangely, the tropical approach to seafood is more complicated than that. For starters, some islands have no seafood at all (believe it or not), surrounded perhaps by poisonous reefs that scare off all finfish and lacking fresh rivers and lakes to support other forms. Residents of some tropical islands must resort to buying all their seafood from foreign boats that tie up at the dock, or from jets that fly in from every corner of the globe.

Tropical seafood, therefore, is partly about ingredients—snapper, for instance, or conch, or the wonderful spiny lobster I like to get from South Africa—but even more often about flavor profiles. Seafood becomes tropical, in many cases, when we cook it with tropical spices and serve it in tropical settings. In the exciting recipes that follow, our shared credo might be expressed: I taste, therefore I am!

Mauritius Fleur de Sel Baked Snapper

1 whole snapper (4 to 5 pounds),
  cleaned, scales on
4 pounds Dominique's Fleur de Sel
  or rock salt
6 egg whites
1 cup extra virgin olive oil
1 tablespoon finely chopped Pickled
  Lemon (recipe on page 143)
1 teaspoon freshly cracked black
  pepper
Mashed potatoes
Lemon slices

These days in restaurants, a lot of chefs are experimenting with "salt-crusted" fish. For one thing, it makes for a dramatic presentation. For another, it keeps the moisture and flavor inside the fish in a way few other techniques can. And using fleur de sel instead of plain salt only makes it better.

Preheat oven to 300°. Dry snapper with a towel and place on a baking sheet. Mix salt and egg whites; spread a 1½-inch layer over the fish. Bake for 1 hour.

Remove from oven and let stand for 5 minutes. Using a knife, remove salt crust; gently peel off skin. Cut through middle of fish, removing bones. Transfer fish to warmed plates; spoon oil over fish. Sprinkle with pickled lemon and pepper. Serve with a side of mashed potatoes and slices of fresh lemon.

Serves 4

Culinary Origins
20° 10' S
57° 30' E

Harvesting fleur de sel on the Indian Ocean island of Mauritius

Red Stripe Clams

Red Stripe Clams

This dish has a lot of flavors going on, including the garam masala that always delivers me to the heart of India. Still, a favorite component of mine has to be the Red Stripe beer from Jamaica. You can use any beer you like, of course. But the swigs of Red Stripe that accompany the cooking will make the cook feel better about the whole enterprise.

In a large sauté pan, heat oil; sauté the shallots, ginger and garlic for 3 minutes. Add beer and rum; cook for 3 minutes. Add clams; cover and cook for 10 minutes. Using a slotted spoon, remove the clams and set aside. Discard any unopened clams.

Stir garam masala, jalapeño and tamarind into the broth. Reduce by one-third. Add butter and scallions. Return clams to the pan; cook for 2 minutes. Add basil and cilantro. Serve clams in warmed soup bowls with plenty of broth.

Serves 4

¼ cup vegetable oil

1 cup finely chopped shallots

2 tablespoons finely chopped fresh ginger

1 tablespoon minced garlic

1 bottle (12 ounces) Red Stripe beer

¼ cup white rum

2 pounds live clams in shells

1 tablespoon Homemade Garam Masala (recipe on page 140)

1 jalapeño pepper, seeded and finely chopped

2 tablespoons Tamarind Purée (recipe on page 146)

2 tablespoons unsalted butter

½ cup finely chopped scallions

1 tablespoon finely chopped fresh basil

1 tablespoon finely chopped fresh cilantro

Culinary Origins
17° 58′ N
76° 48′ W

Yellowtail Snapper
with Shrimp Croquettes

Yellowtail Snapper with Shrimp Croque

1 pound celery root, peeled and
  quartered

1 Yukon Gold potato, peeled

8 cups Chicken Stock
  (recipe on page 148)

1½ pounds raw shrimp, peeled and
  deveined

Salt and freshly ground black pepper
  to taste

1 cup all-purpose flour

6 eggs, beaten

3 cups panko breadcrumbs

4 tablespoons grapeseed oil, *divided*

1 fresh coconut, peeled and cut
  from shell

2 cups Shrimp Stock
  (recipe on page 149)

3 tablespoons light soy sauce

3 tablespoons cilantro juice

3 tablespoons ginger juice

1 tablespoon jalapeño juice

½ tablespoon garlic juice

6 fillets (6 to 7 ounces *each*)
  yellowtail snapper, preferably with
  skin on

Grilled scallops, lump crabmeat *or*
  chopped bok choy for garnish,
  optional

Here is a popular seafood entrée from my restaurant. The seared snapper is certainly the star, but a flavorful croquette and a sauce (or nage) of shrimp and coconut pick up supporting roles.

To make the croquettes, cook the celery root and potato in chicken stock until tender, 35–45 minutes. Cool; purée in a blender or food processor. Add shrimp; purée until incorporated. Season with salt and pepper.

Using a ring mold, form the purée into croquettes; dip in sequence into flour, eggs and breadcrumbs. Heat 2 tablespoons oil in a pan; sauté the croquettes until golden brown, about 2 minutes on each side.

To make the sauce, purée coconut meat in shrimp stock. Add soy sauce and juices; mix well. Heat in a pan but do not boil (to preserve the fresh flavors). In a sauté pan, heat remaining oil; sear the snapper, skin side down, for 6 minutes. Turn and cook 4–6 minutes longer.

To serve, ladle the sauce into shallow bowls; position a croquette on the sauce and lean the snapper against the croquette. Garnish with scallops, crab or bok choy if desired.

Serves 6

Culinary Origins
24° 33' N
81° 46' W

Simple Seared Snapper

Simple Seared Snapper

We're always hearing people tell us that fish dishes should be kept simple, but sometimes even we chefs can forget. This recipe takes that advice to heart, with the seared snapper getting only a drizzle of the wonderful lobster lemon oil.

To make the lobster lemon oil, reduce the stocks over high heat by about three-fourths. Transfer to a blender; slowly add grapeseed oil to emulsify, then add lemon oil.

In a sauté pan, heat vegetable oil; sear the snapper, skin side down, for 3 minutes. Turn and cook 4 minutes longer. To serve, drizzle with lobster lemon oil and sprinkle with tomatoes.

Serves 8

4 cups Lobster Stock
(recipe on page 149)
2 cups Chicken Stock
(recipe on page 148)
1¾ cups grapeseed oil
1 tablespoon lemon oil
1 to 2 tablespoons vegetable oil
8 fillets (6 to 7 ounces *each*)
yellowtail snapper, with skin on
2 tomatoes, peeled and diced

Creole Cobia

Creole Cobia

Now that my home is New Orleans, I love remembering all the other places I've encountered the word "Creole" … in the French Caribbean, in places like Martinique and Guadeloupe, and even far away in the Indian Ocean, where it's used on my home island of Mauritius and nearby Reunion. So this marriage of grilled fish with shrimp and okra is a Creole dish through and through.

In a saucepan over high heat, reduce the shrimp and chicken stocks by one-third. Stir in curry powder; reduce by another third. Transfer to a blender; slowly add grapeseed oil to emulsify. Pour into a saucepan; keep warm.

For the fricassee, in a sauté pan, sauté the okra, shallots, celery and garlic in vegetable oil for 10–12 minutes, until okra is not gluey. Add the tomatoes, tomato paste and stock. Bring to a boil; reduce heat and simmer for 10 minutes. Add shrimp; cook for 2 minutes. Stir in the thyme and jalapeño. Remove from the heat; cover and let stand for 3–4 minutes.

Meanwhile, in a blender, process the vegetable oil, onion, garlic, basil, salt and pepper. Spread over fish; marinate for 5 minutes. Grill for 4 minutes on each side.

On warmed plates, place mounds of shrimp and okra fricassee and jasmine rice side by side, with the cobia on top. Spoon shrimp-curry essence around the edges.

Serves 4

Shrimp-Curry Essence

2 cups Shrimp Stock
(recipe on page 149)

2 cups Chicken Stock
(recipe on page 148)

1 tablespoon Homemade Curry
Powder (recipe on page 140)

¼ cup grapeseed oil

Shrimp and Okra Fricassee

3 cups cut fresh *or* frozen okra

2 shallots, diced

1 rib celery, diced

1 tablespoon minced garlic

1 tablespoon vegetable oil

6 tomatoes, peeled, seeded and diced

1 tablespoon tomato paste

1½ cups Chicken Stock
(recipe on page 148)

½ pound raw small shrimp, peeled

1 teaspoon chopped fresh thyme

1 jalapeño pepper, seeded and diced

¼ cup vegetable oil

¼ onion

2 cloves garlic

4 fresh basil leaves

1 teaspoon sea salt

¼ teaspoon black pepper

4 fillets (6 ounces *each*) fresh Gulf
cobia *or* other firm whitefish

Spiced Jasmine Rice (recipe on page 104)

Louisiana Shrimp with Boniato Galettes

Louisiana Shrimp with Boniato Galette

2 pounds boniato, peeled and cooked

½ pound rock shrimp, peeled

2 red bell peppers, roasted

½ cup reduced shrimp stock

Salt and freshly ground black pepper
   to taste

1 cup all-purpose flour

6 eggs, beaten

1½ cups unseasoned breadcrumbs

4 tablespoons vegetable oil, *divided*

60 raw jumbo shrimp, peeled and
   deveined

Culinary Origins
29° 57' N
90° 4' W

Boniato is yet another of those tropical starches, the kind of strange shapes and sizes that fills every island waterfront market when the whole village converges once or twice a week. The vendors call out their wares in singsong voices, and the women load up their handwoven baskets and carry their groceries home balanced atop their heads. Yes, I think of all those memories every time I prepare this dish!

Purée the boniato, rock shrimp and roasted peppers; place in a bowl. Stir in the stock; season with salt and pepper. Using an ice cream scoop or your hands, form the mixture into balls; roll in sequence in flour, eggs and breadcrumbs. Press each ball into a ring to form a small tower, then lift off the ring.

Preheat oven to 180°. Sear the galettes in a sauté pan with 2 tablespoons oil; place in the oven for 10–12 minutes. Meanwhile, pan-sear the shrimp in remaining oil. Arrange six shrimp and one galette on each plate.

Serves 10

Cracked Conch with Cho-Cho Risotto

Cracked Conch with Cho-Cho Risotto

In New Orleans, we tend to think we invented the mirliton, stuffing the vegetable with crabmeat, chopped shrimp and breadcrumbs and baking it till tender. But actually, people all over the world love mirlitons, calling them by names as varied as chayote, vegetable pear and christophene. On a lot of islands, the name gets shortened to cho-cho.

To make the risotto, in a saucepan, sauté the onion and garlic in olive oil until they start to turn golden. Add corn; cook 2 minutes longer. Add rice; stir to coat with oil. Cook and stir for 2 minutes over medium-high heat. Add wine and cook until almost evaporated. Reduce heat; gradually add hot stock and cream, stirring until absorbed. Cook for 15–20 minutes or until rice is al dente, stirring occasionally.

Julienne one mirliton and set aside. Finely chop the remaining mirlitons; add to risotto. Season with salt and pepper. Toss the julienned mirliton with tomatoes and mojo. In a sauté pan, heat vegetable oil and butter; sauté the conch for 1 minute on each side.

To serve, spoon risotto into a ring mold; remove ring. Top with three pieces of sautéed conch and then the mirliton-tomato relish.

Serves 10

1 onion, finely chopped

4 cloves garlic, minced

2 tablespoons olive oil

Kernels from 4 ears fresh corn

3 cups Arborio rice

½ cup dry white wine

6 cups Lobster Stock
    (recipe on page 149), heated

1 cup heavy cream

3 mirlitons

Salt and black pepper to taste

2 tomatoes, peeled and diced

3 tablespoons Grapefruit and Scotch
    Bonnet Mojo (recipe on page 145)

30 farm-raised whole baby conch

2 tablespoons vegetable oil

1 tablespoon butter

Culinary Origins
23° 7′ N – 10° 38′ N
82° 21′ W – 61° 31′ W

Mojito Grilled Scallops

¼ cup unsalted butter

4 green onions, finely chopped

1 teaspoon minced garlic

¼ cup light rum

¼ cup plus 2 tablespoons fresh lime juice, *divided*

¼ cup finely chopped fresh mint

1 teaspoon sugar

Salt and freshly ground black pepper to taste

18 large sea scallops

Every once in a while, I taste a popular cocktail and think of some way to apply its flavors to food. So it goes with these Mojito scallops, named and patterned about Cuba's beloved twist on the Deep South mint julep ... or was it vice versa?

In a saucepan, melt butter; sauté the green onions and garlic until lightly caramelized. Add the rum, ¼ cup lime juice, mint and sugar. Bring to a boil; cook until reduced, about 5 minutes. Season with salt and pepper.

Grill the scallops just until done, about 3 minutes on each side, brushing lightly with the remaining lime juice as they cook. Spoon the mojito sauce onto six plates; top with three scallops each.

Serves 6

Shrimp Skewers with Tamarind Butter

Shrimp Skewers with Tamarind Butter

The taste of the tropical fruit called tamarind is hard to describe ... but as with, say, truffles much farther north, once you taste it, you'll know whenever it comes near. I think it's perfect in the butter that accompanies these grilled shrimp.

Place shrimp in a large bowl; stir in orange juice and coconut oil. Cover and marinate in the refrigerator overnight.

In a mixing bowl, whip the butter with a whisk until light and fluffy. Dissolve the tamarind in water; stir into the butter. Add coconut flakes, salt and pepper. Refrigerate overnight.

About 3 hours before serving, remove tamarind butter from the refrigerator to soften. Shortly before serving, skewer the shrimp on 12 soaked bamboo skewers; grill just until pink. Place two skewers on each plate with a small bowl of tamarind butter for dipping.

Serves 6

2 pounds raw large shrimp, peeled and deveined
1 cup freshly squeezed orange juice
1 cup coconut oil
1 pound butter, softened
¼ cup Tamarind Purée (recipe on page 146)
2 tablespoons water
¼ cup unsweetened dried coconut flakes, toasted
Salt and freshly ground black pepper to taste

Culinary Origins
23° 7' N – 10° 38' N
82° 21' W – 61° 31' W

Sweet-Hot Swordfish en Brochette

Sweet-Hot Swordfish en Brochette

Like the tropical Asian cuisines they link with so comfortably, Caribbean dishes often come down to a balance of sweet and hot. In fact, ask any Caribbean cook about "sweet and hot," and you'll surely hear something suggestive, as though all pleasures are connected in the islands. Even as just one pleasure, this shish kebab of sweet-hot swordfish is certain to please.

In a saucepan, sauté the onion, scallions and garlic in oil until softened, about 4 minutes. Add pineapple and rum; cook for 3 minutes. Cool; purée in a blender. Add Scotch bonnet, cilantro and mint; mix well.

Cut the pineapple, onion and bell peppers into similar-size chunks; thread alternately with swordfish onto skewers. Place in a large shallow pan; pour marinade over skewers. Refrigerate for 30 minutes. Grill over medium heat for 10 minutes, turning to cook evenly.

Serves 4

Marinade

1 yellow onion, diced

3 scallions, chopped

4 cloves garlic, minced

2 tablespoons vegetable oil

½ pineapple, peeled, cored and diced

¼ cup dark rum

½ Scotch bonnet pepper, seeded and diced

2 tablespoons chopped fresh cilantro

1 teaspoon chopped fresh mint

Skewers

½ pineapple

1 red onion

1 green bell pepper

1 red bell pepper

1 yellow bell pepper

3 pounds fresh swordfish, cut into 1-inch cubes

Culinary Origins

41° 25' N

2° 10' E

Lobster Rougail

20 ripe Roma tomatoes

¼ cup olive oil

2 yellow onions, finely chopped

6 cloves garlic, minced

1 piece fresh ginger (2 inches), diced

½ teaspoon Homemade Garam
   Masala (recipe on page 140)

½ teaspoon ground turmeric

4 curry leaves

2 tablespoons chopped fresh parsley

2 tablespoons chopped fresh thyme

Salt and freshly ground black pepper
   to taste

6 uncooked spiny lobster tails

Steamed basmati *or* jasmine rice

Every family on the island of Mauritius cooks rougail at least once a week. It's one of those dishes that arrived with one ethnic group—in this case, the many Indian immigrants—but came to belong to us all.

Culinary Origins
20° 10′ S
57° 30′ E

Grill the tomatoes until the skin starts to blister; peel. Purée the pulp until smooth; set aside. In a large sauté pan, heat oil; sauté the onions until golden. Stir in garlic and ginger. Add garam masala and turmeric; cook and stir for 3 minutes. Add the tomato purée and curry leaves; cook for 5 minutes. Stir in the parsley and thyme. Season with salt and pepper; simmer 5 minutes longer.

Pan-roast the lobster tails in batches until the meat can be removed whole from the shell. Finish cooking the meat in the pan, then return to the shells. Reheat the rougail in the lobster pan to retrieve the lobster cooking juices. Serve each lobster tail with rice and generous spoonfuls of rougail.

Serves 6–8

Bahian Lobster Moqueca

Bahian Lobster Moqueca

This dish won't win any "light cooking" awards, but it is intense and exotic in flavor. It hails from the beach-fronted Bahia region of Brazil, the area most influenced by its large population of African slaves.

Remove lobster from the shell and cut the meat into bite-size chunks. Place in a bowl; cover with lime juice. Season with salt and pepper; set aside. In a large saucepan, heat vegetable oil; sauté the onions, bell peppers, Scotch bonnet and cumin until onions are soft. Add lobster with lime juice, stirring briefly to coat the meat.

   Add tomatoes, cilantro, coconut flakes and milk. Bring to a boil; cook until thickened, about 10 minutes. Add dende oil; cook 3 minutes longer. To serve, spoon the lobster chunks and sauce over rice; garnish with cilantro.

Serves 4–6

1 lobster (1½ to 2 pounds), steamed
   in the shell
Juice of 3 limes
Salt and freshly ground black pepper
   to taste
2 tablespoons vegetable oil
2 yellow onions, finely chopped
4 green onions, finely chopped
2 green bell peppers, finely chopped
1 Scotch bonnet pepper
1 teaspoon ground cumin
2 cups chopped tomatoes with juice
¼ cup chopped fresh cilantro
¾ cup unsweetened dried coconut
   flakes
½ cup Coconut Milk
   (recipe on page 147)
¼ cup dende (red palm) oil
Steamed rice
Additional chopped cilantro

Culinary Origins
8° 6′ S
34° 53′ W

Summertime Fish Salad

Summertime Fish Salad

1 cup fresh pineapple juice

¼ cup fresh lime juice

1 tablespoon malt vinegar

2 cloves garlic

1 Serrano pepper, seeded

15 fresh cilantro leaves

1½ cups peanut oil

Salt and freshly ground black pepper
    to taste

3 pounds snapper fillets

3 cups julienned jicama

1½ cups julienned carrots

3 scallions, chopped

2 cups hearts of romaine

Few things are better in the summertime—or just about anytime on many islands—than a refreshing seafood salad. Actually, you can cook the seafood any way you prefer, but I think the light grilled taste imparts a wonderful additional layer to the flavors.

To make the dressing, combine the juices, vinegar, garlic, Serrano and cilantro in a blender until smooth. With the blender running, slowly add oil until incorporated. Season with salt and pepper.

Grill the snapper until lightly striped but not overcooked. Shred into bite-size pieces with a fork. In a large bowl, combine the fish, jicama, carrots and scallions; add dressing and toss. Let stand for 10–15 minutes. Arrange hearts of romaine on plates; mound the salad in the center.

Serves 6

Roasted Whole Red Snapper

Although cooking fish whole offers considerable advantages in terms of flavor, surely the biggest advantage is the "Wow" you hear when this platter reaches the table. And considering how they're cooked, don't forget to eat your vegetables!

4 whole red snapper (1 to 1½ pounds *each*), cleaned
½ cup fresh lime juice
Salt and freshly ground black pepper to taste
½ cup olive oil
1 large onion, thinly sliced
2 carrots, sliced
1 cup chopped callaloo *or* kale
1 Scotch bonnet pepper, seeded and chopped
1 tablespoon chopped fresh parsley
1 teaspoon minced garlic
½ teaspoon chopped fresh thyme
½ teaspoon chopped fresh oregano
1 bay leaf

Rub the snapper inside and out with lime juice; season with salt and pepper. Marinate for 30 minutes.

Preheat oven to 400°. In a large roasting pan, heat oil on the stovetop. Add the remaining ingredients; sauté until lightly caramelized, about 5 minutes. Then spread vegetables and herbs evenly across the bottom of the pan; top with snapper. Roast, uncovered, for 30 minutes or until fish flakes easily.

Transfer the vegetables to a serving platter; remove bay leaf. Top with whole snapper.

Serves 4

Meat of the Matter

4

s a rule of thumb, the tropics enjoy more meat and enjoy it more often than most outsiders would expect. For one thing, the presumption is that warm weather makes people want to eat meat less and perhaps lighter seafood more, a valid concept in a place with all four seasons but not in a world of nearly eternal sunshine. Meat eating in the tropics is a matter of both taste and tradition, with many surprisingly rich stews and braises turning up when you're expecting only a lime-kissed seafood salad.

In addition, meat cookery abounds on tropical islands because (within the limits of affordability) it abounded in the cultures that fed the islands with immigrants over the centuries. Evolution occurred, of course, most strikingly when the curried lamb cherished by laborers from India became the more readily available curried goat in the Caribbean. Pork may well be the favored meat on most islands, particularly those settled by the Spanish, but these days any and all meats may be enjoyed somewhere in the tropics.

Mauritian Chicken Roti

Mauritian Chicken Roti

Here's one of the best recipes I remember my mother making when I was small … a clear testament to the Indian contribution to Mauritian cuisine. One of the best parts is the grilled roti bread we called farata.

In a large pot, heat vegetable oil; sauté the onion, garlic, Scotch bonnet and garam masala until lightly caramelized. Add chicken; cook for 5–7 minutes or until browned. Add stock; cover and simmer for 45 minutes or until chicken is tender.

Meanwhile, prepare the farata. In a mixing bowl, combine the flour, salt, water and 2 tablespoons olive oil. Divide the dough into four balls. Cover with plastic wrap and let stand in a cool place for 30 minutes.

Remove chicken pieces from sauce; when cool enough to handle, remove meat from bones. Return meat to the sauce; cook until thickened, about 10–15 minutes.

Roll out each ball of dough to form a square about ¼ inch thick. Brush with remaining olive oil; grill until golden brown. Spoon chicken and sauce onto each farata; roll up.

Serves 8

2 tablespoons vegetable oil
1 yellow onion, chopped
4 cloves garlic, minced
1 Scotch bonnet pepper, seeded and chopped
3 tablespoons Homemade Garam Masala (recipe on page 140)
1 chicken (2 to 3 pounds), cut up
4 cups Chicken Stock (recipe on page 148)

Farata
3 cups all-purpose flour
2 tablespoons salt
2 cups lukewarm water
¼ cup olive oil, *divided*

Culinary Origins
20° 10' S
57° 30' E

Balinese Satay

6 shallots, peeled

3 pieces lemongrass

2 cloves garlic

1 tablespoon fresh cilantro leaves

2 tablespoons vegetable oil

2 chicken legs and thighs, deboned and cut into serving-size pieces

3 tablespoons sugar

1 teaspoon ground turmeric

½ teaspoon crushed red pepper

½ teaspoon salt

Nasi Goreng

2 tablespoons vegetable oil

1 cup cubed pork

1 yellow onion, diced

2 cloves garlic, minced

1 teaspoon finely chopped fresh ginger

1 jalapeño pepper, seeded and diced

1 cup finely chopped carrots

1 cup finely chopped green bell pepper

1 cup finely chopped red bell pepper

1 cup chopped peeled raw shrimp

4 eggs, beaten

4 cups cooked white rice, chilled

¼ to ½ cup soy sauce

Cashew Nut Chutney

1 cup cashews

1 teaspoon peanut oil

1 yellow onion, quartered

1 jalapeño pepper, stem removed

1 clove garlic

8 fresh mint leaves

4 fresh bay leaves

3 tablespoons Tamarind Purée (recipe on page 146)

Sea salt

In a food processor, make a paste of the shallots, lemongrass, garlic, cilantro and oil. Place chicken in a bowl; stir in the paste, sugar, turmeric, red pepper and salt. Cover and refrigerate for 12 hours.

In a wok, heat oil; brown pork cubes. Add the onion, garlic, ginger, jalapeño, carrots and bell peppers; stir-fry until softened. Stir in the shrimp, then the beaten eggs. Fold vigorously into the mixture like an omelet. While eggs are still a little runny, add rice and soy sauce. Turn with a spatula to thoroughly combine; cook until the rice begins to crackle and pop.

For the chutney, lightly fry cashews in peanut oil, then purée with the remaining ingredients.

When ready to serve, thread chicken onto 16 soaked bamboo skewers; grill for 4–5 minutes or until no longer pink. Fry eight eggs sunny-side up. Mound the Nasi Goreng on plates, using a bowl for shape; top each with a fried egg. Arrange two skewers of satay around the rice.

Serves 8

Satay is Indonesia's answer to the global tradition of skewering meat and seafood. Nasi Goreng is the chain of island's answer to Chinese fried rice, made "special" on the beautiful isle of Bali by the addition of a fried egg on top. In Bali, this is a popular breakfast. In the United States, it's probably more likely to be lunch.

Culinary Origins
8° 39′ S
115° 13′ E

South African Chicken

South African Chicken

Like most of my favorite parts of the world, South Africa offers a rich mélange of cultural influences. This dish draws heat from the African tradition of peri-peri (actually a type of pepper, but now a hot sauce or even a style of cooking), then deals with the heat as Indians often do, with a cooling cucumber-yogurt sauce.

3 cups Peri-Peri Sauce (recipe on page 141)
½ cup chopped fresh cilantro
½ cup chopped fresh basil
2 jalapeño peppers, seeded
1 tablespoon Homemade Garam Masala
   (recipe on page 140)
1 chicken (2 pounds), cut into 8 pieces
Spiced Jasmine Rice (recipe on page 104)
Sauce Raita (recipe on page 145)

In a blender, combine peri-peri sauce, cilantro, basil, jalapeños and garam masala; make a smooth purée. Spread about half of the marinade over chicken pieces; refrigerate for 4 hours.

Preheat oven to 350°. Grill chicken over medium heat for 10 minutes. Cover with the remaining marinade; finish in the oven for 20–25 minutes. Serve two pieces of chicken per person with rice and raita.

Serves 4

Curried Goat in a Bread Bowl

Curried Goat in a Bread Bowl

One of the most interesting and important groups of immigrants to enrich islands around the world, including my home of Mauritius, is made up of workers from India. This dish reflects the flavor profile of an Indian curry, along with the need to use whatever meat is available. Goat is surprisingly delicious and tender.

2 tablespoons vegetable oil

1½ pounds goat meat, trimmed and cubed

3 large yellow onions, diced

3 cloves garlic, minced

3 tablespoons Homemade Curry Powder (recipe on page 140)

2 large potatoes, peeled and cubed

3 tomatoes, diced

3 cups Chicken Stock (recipe on page 148)

1 tablespoon wine vinegar

1 teaspoon salt

1 bay leaf

4 small loaves rustic bread

In a large pan, heat oil; brown the meat in batches. In the same pan, sauté onions and garlic until soft. Add curry powder and stir for 1 minute. Add potatoes; cook and stir to cover with curry. Add the tomatoes, stock, vinegar and salt. Return meat to the pan. Cover and simmer for 1½ hours.

Add bay leaf; simmer 30 minutes longer or until the meat is tender. Remove the bay leaf. Hollow out loaves of bread; fill with meat mixture. Serve hot.

Serves 4

Sugarcane-Skewered Sweetbreads

Sugarcane-Skewered Sweetbreads

Here's a dish that has became a signature of mine, and it's been one that has convinced a lot of timid first-timers that sweetbreads are wonderful. The important thing, beyond the clever presentation on sugarcane skewers, is to braise and then brown the sweetbreads as directed. I think you'll love the texture.

Wash the sweetbreads under cold running water for 30 minutes. In a large pot, bring stock to a boil. Add sweetbreads; reduce heat and poach for 5 minutes. Remove the sweetbreads and place on a tray. Top with another tray and place a weight on top. Wrap in plastic wrap and press overnight in the refrigerator. Refrigerate veal stock for later use.

To prepare the fritters, cook lentils in water for 25 minutes; drain. In a sauté pan, heat olive oil; sauté the corn, onion and garlic until golden, about 2 minutes. Add garam masala and lentils; simmer for 2 minutes. Purée in a food processor with potatoes. Season with salt and pepper.

Using a pastry bag, pipe the purée and cut into 3-inch lengths. In sequence, dredge fritters in flour, eggs and breadcrumbs. Heat vegetable oil to 370°; fry the fritters until golden on all sides, about 6 minutes per batch.

Blanch the parsley in water for 3–5 seconds; cool quickly by placing in cold water. Purée parsley with olive oil; strain through cheesecloth.

Cut sweetbreads into eight pieces; skewer on sugarcane strips. In a sauté pan, heat vegetable oil; sauté sweetbread skewers until golden brown on all sides, about 5 minutes. Reduce the veal stock over high heat by one-third.

To serve, set fritters in the center of a warmed plate; lean a sweetbread skewer against each fritter. Drizzle with warmed veal stock and parsley oil.

Serves 8

3 pounds veal sweetbreads
 (preferably Kobe)
6 cups Veal Stock
 (recipe on page 148)
Spiced Lentil-White Corn Fritters
3 cups black lentils
6 cups water
½ tablespoon olive oil
Kernels from 2 ears white corn
¼ cup finely chopped onion
1 clove garlic, minced
½ teaspoon Homemade Garam
 Masala (recipe on page 140)
1 cup mashed potatoes
Salt and freshly ground black pepper
 to taste
1 cup all-purpose flour
3 eggs, beaten
2 cups unseasoned breadcrumbs
3 cups vegetable oil for deep-frying

1 bunch fresh parsley
7 cups water
2 cups olive oil
8 thin strips raw sugarcane *or*
 bamboo skewers
2 tablespoons vegetable oil

Thyme-Roasted Cornish Hens with Breadfruit Chips

Thyme-Roasted Cornish Hens with Bread

The idea of serving chicken with store-bought potato chips is not worth considering, but when we dream up homemade breadfruit chips, the combination gets intriguing indeed. Plus, I love cooking "potato dishes" with breadfruit, since immigrants to the islands had to use breadfruit because they had no so-called "Irish potatoes." In other words, their necessity becomes our invention.

Run the hens inside and out with limes. In a blender, purée the onion, garlic, thyme, olive oil, vinegar and mustard. Rub over hens. Refrigerate for at least 2 hours or overnight.

Slice breadfruit lengthwise into thick wedges; soak in heavily salted water for 1 hour.

Preheat oven to 400°. Place the hens in a shallow roasting pan. Bake for 15 minutes. Reduce oven temperature to 350°. Bake 15–20 minutes longer or until juices run clear. Deglaze the pan with wine, stirring to scrape up browned bits and create a sauce.

Heat vegetable or peanut oil to 370°. Pat breadfruit dry with paper towels; fry wedges in oil, a few at a time, until cooked through. Drain on paper towels.

Serve hens drizzled with sauce. Garnish with breadfruit chips and thyme sprigs.

Serves 4

4 Cornish hens *or* small roasting
  chickens
4 fresh limes, sliced
1 yellow onion, quartered
3 cloves garlic
2 teaspoons fresh thyme leaves
3 tablespoons olive oil
1 tablespoon red wine vinegar
1 teaspoon prepared mustard
1 green to semi-ripe breadfruit,
  peeled and quartered
Vegetable *or* peanut oil for deep-frying
½ cup dry white wine
Fresh thyme sprigs for garnish

Culinary Origins
23° 7′ N – 10° 38′ N
82° 21′ W – 61° 31′ W

Chimichurri Pork Chops
with Pork Confit-Yucca Fritters

Chimichurri Pork Chops with Pork Confit

2 tablespoons minced garlic

1 tablespoon chopped fresh thyme

1 teaspoon cumin

1 teaspoon ground coriander

2 pounds pork butt

5 pounds rendered pork fat

8 thick-cut pork chops

1½ cups Oven-Dried Tomato
    Chimichurri (recipe on page 144)

2 pounds yucca, boiled and puréed

Salt and freshly ground black pepper
    to taste

1 cup all-purpose flour

2 eggs, lightly beaten

3 cups unseasoned breadcrumbs

Culinary Origins
34° 40' S
58° 30' W

I've always been fascinated with plates that combine several versions of the same meat. On my menu, studies of things like lamb and duck abound. You might say I'm doing that in a smaller way with pork in this dish, which contrasts the terrific flavor of pork chops with fritters combining shredded pork butt and starchy yucca.

Combine the garlic, thyme, cumin and coriander; rub over pork butt. Refrigerate for 12 hours.

Preheat oven to 200°. In a roasting pan, combine pork butt with rendered fat. Bake for 3½ hours. Meanwhile, marinate pork chops in chimichurri for 2 hours.

When pork butt is tender, remove from the fat and reserve the fat. Shred pork with a fork and combine thoroughly with yucca purée. Season with salt and pepper. Using a ring mold, form pork-yucca mixture into fritters; dredge in sequence in flour, eggs and breadcrumbs. Heat the reserved pork fat in a pan; fry fritters until golden brown, about 5 minutes per batch.

Grill the pork chops for 8 minutes on each side for medium. Serve with fritters.

Serves 8

Braised Pork Belly and Breadfruit Escabèche

Braised Pork Belly and Breadfruit Es

1 pork belly (5 pounds, preferably karabuta)

4 cups Chicken Stock (recipe on page 148)

3 pounds breadfruit, peeled and cubed

4 cups boiling water

8 small additional breadfruit

1 yellow onion, finely chopped

1 teaspoon minced garlic

¼ teaspoon minced fresh ginger

1 teaspoon Homemade Curry Powder (recipes on page 140)

1 teaspoon allspice berries

½ cup white vinegar

Salt and freshly ground black pepper to taste

Smothered Callaloo

1 cup unsalted butter

2 cups chopped onion

1 cup chopped celery

1 teaspoon minced garlic

1 Scotch bonnet pepper, finely chopped

2 bunches fresh callaloo *or* kale

1 tablespoon salt

½ teaspoon coarsely ground black pepper

Karabuta pork is sometimes called "Kobe pork," since it follows the methods pioneered in Japan that give us the world's more tender (and most expensive) beef. Not too many Americans have cooked and eaten pork belly in recent years, but its joys are being rediscovered by chefs and more adventurous diners all over the country.

Preheat oven to 225°. Place whole pork belly in a roasting pan; add stock. Braise in the oven until tender, about 1½ hours. In a large saucepan, partially cook breadfruit cubes in boiling water for 6 minutes; drain and set aside. Hollow out additional breadfruit to serve as "bowls;" set aside.

Remove pork belly from braising liquid; set liquid aside. Cut pork into 1-inch squares. In a sauté pan, sear the squares on all sides to render the fat. Add the onion, garlic, ginger, curry powder and allspice; stir for 1 minute. Add vinegar. Reduce heat; simmer pork in this "escabèche" for 15 minutes Add the breadfruit cubes; simmer 10 minutes longer. Season with salt and pepper. Remove from the heat; keep warm.

In a large saucepan, melt butter; sauté the onion, celery, garlic and Scotch bonnet until lightly caramelized. Add callaloo; sauté until lightly browned, 15–20 minutes. Add salt, pepper and reserved braising liquid. Simmer until callaloo is tender and liquid is almost gone, about 30 minutes, stirring occasionally to prevent sticking.

Spoon pork and breadfruit mixture into breadfruit bowls. Serve smothered callaloo on the side.

Serves 8

Gaucho Beef Fillets

Gaucho Beef Fillets

Like just about everybody, I love a good fillet. But I especially love it with a filling of seasoned cheese—the French herb-kissed Boursin is a favorite. In this dish, we take Boursin on a southern vacation, spicing up cream cheese with the chimichurri sauce Americans have learned to love at steakhouses themed around the "gaucho country" of Argentina and southern Brazil. I like to serve this dish with potato pancakes or carrot flan.

In a large pot, reduce the veal stock with thyme by about two-thirds. In a separate pot, sauté shallots in olive oil until caramelized; add wine and reduce by four-fifths. Strain the stock and add to the shallots; reduce by a further fifth. Skim off excess fat; keep warm.

In a food processor, purée the parsley, garlic, oregano, peppers, olive oil and cream cheese until smooth. Season with salt and pepper. Cut a slit in each fillet and fill with cream cheese mixture.

Preheat oven to 425°. Rub fillets with vegetable oil; season with salt and pepper. Brown on both sides in a preheated pan, then place in the oven until meat reaches desired doneness (7 minutes for rare to about 12 minutes for medium). Serve on warmed dinner plates, with shallot jus spooned over the top.

Serves 10

Shallot Jus

8 cups Veal Stock (recipe on page 148)
¼ bunch fresh thyme
10 shallots, thinly sliced
1 tablespoon olive oil
1 bottle red wine

Chimichurri Cream Cheese

½ bunch fresh parsley
2 cloves garlic
½ tablespoon chopped fresh oregano
½ tablespoon crushed red pepper
½ tablespoon ground chimayo pepper
¼ cup olive oil
1 cup cream cheese
Salt and freshly ground black pepper to taste

10 beef fillets (8 ounces *each*, preferably center cut)
¼ cup vegetable oil

Culinary Origins
34° 40' S
58° 30' W

Braised Short Ribs with Debris Cakes

Braised Short Ribs with Debris Cakes

8 beef short ribs (4 ounces *each*)

2 tablespoons olive oil

2 carrots, roughly chopped

3 ribs celery, roughly chopped

1 yellow onion, roughly chopped

1 bottle dry red wine

4 cups Veal Stock (recipe on page 148)

Butternut Squash Debris Cakes

2 butternut squash

Salt and freshly ground black pepper
    to taste

1 cup all-purpose flour

3 eggs, beaten

3 cups unseasoned breadcrumbs

¼ cup vegetable oil

Watercress Salad

1 cup olive oil

2 tablespoons sherry vinegar

1 tablespoon Dijon mustard

Salt and freshly ground black pepper
    to taste

2 bunches watercress

Dominique's Fleur de Sel

Short ribs have really found an audience in recent years, but I think merely dousing them with bottled barbecue sauce disguises some of their finest qualities. My version involves braising them till the meat is fall-off-the-bone tender in red wine, then using the "debris" from the pan (as we say in New Orleans) to makes cakes with butternut squash.

Preheat oven to 250°. In a large pan, sear ribs in olive oil on all sides until golden brown. Remove ribs. Add carrots, celery and onion; sauté for 4 minutes. Add wine; reduce by half. Add stock; bring to a boil. Remove from the heat; add ribs. Cover with foil. Bake until very tender, about 4 hours. Remove from the oven. Reserve 1 cup of "debris" (browned bits of beef from bottom of pan). Set ribs aside.

Increase oven temperature to 350°. Bake the squash for 30 minutes; cool. Scoop out pulp and purée; combine with reserved beef debris, using as little pan juice as possible. Season with salt and pepper. Press the mixture into a 2-inch ring mold to form little "towers." Dust the cakes in flour, then coat with eggs and breadcrumbs. Heat vegetable oil in a pan; brown cakes until golden, turning until sides are uniform. Finish for 5 minutes in the oven.

Strain cooking juices from ribs; reduce over high heat by about one-third. Return ribs to pan; slowly heat for 3 minutes before serving. Meanwhile, in a bowl, whisk the olive oil, vinegar, mustard, salt and pepper; toss with watercress.

Place debris cakes on plates; divide watercress salad over the top. Place one short rib with sauce alongside each cake. Sprinkle ribs with fleur de sel.

Serves 8

Island-Rubbed Steak

Island-Rubbed Steak

Instead of the marinade used in our early dishes inspired by Jamaican jerk, this wonderful steak draws interest from a paste that combines fresh and dried seasonings. The result will impress anyone you happen to be cooking for. As always, I opt for "heat" at the lower end, since that's what most people like. But certainly there's more than one Scotch bonnet in this world.

Roast allspice berries in a 300° oven for 7 minutes. With a mortar and pestle, crush berries into a powder. Add the green onions, cilantro, bay leaves, garlic, Scotch bonnet, thyme, salt and pepper; crush thoroughly to make a paste. Rub over flank steaks. Refrigerate for 24 hours.

Grill steaks over medium heat for about 8 minutes for medium-rare. Thinly slice across the grain.

Serves 8

4 tablespoons allspice berries

1½ cups chopped green onions

¼ cup fresh cilantro leaves

4 bay leaves, stalk removed and chopped

2 cloves garlic

1 Scotch bonnet pepper, seeds removed

2 tablespoons chopped fresh thyme

Salt and freshly ground black pepper to taste

3½ pounds flank steaks

Culinary Origins
23° 7′ N – 10° 38′ N
82° 21′ W – 61° 31′ W

Trio of Lamb
Trio of Lamb

Here is one of the most popular meat entrees at Dominique's—a dish with not one, not two, but three variations on the same meat. The recipe requires some time and care, as you can see, but the bulk of steps can be spread out over a day or two. That way you'll have the energy (and calm) to enjoy your own dinner party.

With a mandoline, thinly slice potatoes and malanga. Fry in fat until almost cooked through but not crispy. Line a terrine mold with plastic wrap; line with some of the bacon slices. Mix goat cheese and thyme; transfer to a pastry bag.

Place potato and malanga slices over bacon in bottom of terrine; spread with lamb confit and then the goat cheese mixture. Layer with the remaining potato and malanga slices. Cover with remaining bacon and then with plastic wrap. Place lid on terrine mold.

Refrigerate if making the day ahead. Or preheat oven to 350° and bake for 30 minutes. Remove from oven and press out excess bacon fat.

Mix ground lamb with thyme, rosemary and harissa. Wash and open the casing under running water. Fill a cookie press with the meat mixture and press about 5 inches into the casing. Turn off press and twist the casing to seal, tying each end with twine. Repeat until all meat is used. Cut sausages apart at twists with scissors. In a pan, heat oil to very hot; brown sausage on all sides. Reduce heat; cook about 5 minutes longer or until cooked through.

Increase oven temperature to 375°. Season the rack of lamb with salt and pepper. Sear on both sides in a pan over medium-high heat for about 5 minutes. Cool. Brush with mustard; press thyme into mustard. Roast the lamb until medium-rare, about 20 minutes. Let stand for 3 minutes before cutting into chops. Serve a chop with a slice of terrine and a section of merquez sausage.

Serves 8

Terrine
1 pound Idaho potatoes, peeled
1 pound malanga, peeled
5 quarts lamb *or* duck fat
14 ounces sliced bacon
12 ounces goat cheese
2 tablespoons chopped fresh thyme
1 pound lamb confit, minced

Merquez Sausage
1 pound ground lamb (with at least 15% fat)
1 tablespoon chopped fresh thyme
1 tablespoon chopped fresh rosemary
½ cup Harissa (recipe on page 144)
4 feet of lamb casing (ask your butcher)
1 tablespoon olive oil

Rack of Lamb
1 rack of lamb (4 pounds)
Sea salt and freshly ground black pepper to taste
2 tablespoons Dijon mustard
¼ cup chopped fresh thyme

Jerk-Marinated Roast Leg of Lamb

Jerk-Marinated Roast Leg of Lamb

The culinary concept of "jerk" comes to us from Jamaica and shares the same Spanish root word for smoking meats that gives us beef jerky. Yet even as Jamaican "jerk pork," there is no similarity to the jerky you can buy beside the cash register at gas stations and truck stops. The process delivers tender, still juicy meat, especially when our jerk marinade is applied to a leg of young lamb.

1 boneless leg of lamb (5 to 7 pounds), butterflied
5 cups Jerk Marinade (recipe on page 141), *divided*
1 cup peanut oil
Double recipe of Spiced Jasmine Rice (recipe on page 104)
Sauce Raita (recipe on page 145)

Cover lamb thoroughly with 3 cups marinade; spread the meat open on a tray lined with plastic wrap. Place another tray lined with plastic wrap on top; set a weight on top to press the meat down. Refrigerate overnight.

Preheat oven to 325°. Remove lamb from marinade; roll up and tie with kitchen string. Heat oil in a large pan; brown the meat until golden on all sides, about 10 minutes. Place in a shallow roasting pan; brush with remaining marinade. Bake until medium-rare, about 1½ hours. Let stand for 10 minutes before removing string and carving. Serve with rice and sauce.

Serves 12–14

Jerk Pork Tenderloin

Jerk Pork Tenderloin

This is closer to original jerk pork in Jamaica than the leg of lamb at left. In fact, it's one of the most easily accessible ways for Americans to enjoy the "joys of jerk" without any of the beach or roadside smoking paraphernalia you see every time you turn around in the islands. As with chutney in Indian dishes, the jicama-grapefruit slaw provides a nice zing while cooling your mouth from the hot peppers.

Cut pork tenderloin into eight equal pieces. In a blender or food processor, combine the next 11 ingredients. Rub over pork. Refrigerate for 2 hours.

In a bowl, combine the slaw ingredients; refrigerate until serving. Grill the pork until medium, about 8 minutes (be careful not to overcook; it should be moist). Place the slaw in the middle of each plate and place the pork on top.

Serves 8

2 pounds pork tenderloin

1 yellow onion, quartered

²/₃ cup chopped green onions

2 Scotch bonnet peppers, seeded

2 teaspoons chopped fresh thyme

2 teaspoons ground cinnamon

1½ teaspoons salt

1½ teaspoons freshly ground black pepper

1 teaspoon ground allspice

¼ teaspoon ground nutmeg

¼ cup vegetable oil

1 tablespoon dark rum

Jicama-Grapefruit Slaw

2 pounds jicama root, peeled and thinly sliced

2 grapefruit, peeled and diced

1 tablespoon ginger juice

1 tablespoon finely chopped fresh mint

1 tablespoon finely chopped fresh cilantro

Culinary Origins
17° 58' N
76° 48' W

Beef Medallions
with Rum-Butter Mushroom Sauce

Beef Medallions with Rum-Butter Mus

2 tablespoons unsalted butter

2 tablespoons finely chopped onion

1 teaspoon minced garlic

1 cup sliced morel *or* white
   mushrooms

1 cup Beef Stock
   (recipe on page 148)

½ cup dark rum

½ cup heavy cream

1 teaspoon Dijon mustard

8 beef tenderloin medallions
   (3 ounces *each*)

Salt and freshly ground black pepper
   to taste

Old Europe is full of recipes along these lines, some going the extra mile by being flamed with cognac tableside. The tropical New World looked longingly at such classics, re-creating them a thousand different ways with their spirit of convenience and choice, rum.

Melt butter in a saucepan; sauté the onion and garlic until lightly caramelized. Add mushrooms; cook until softened, 2–3 minutes. Stir in the stock, rum, cream and mustard. Bring to a boil; reduce until sauce coats the back of a spoon, 2–3 minutes.

   Season beef medallions with salt and pepper. Cook either under a broiler or in a heavy skillet, turning once, until meat reaches desired doneness. Serve two medallions per person, with mushroom sauce spooned over the top and sides.

Serves 4

Oxtail and Broad Beans

Oxtail and Broad Beans

This dish seems almost Tuscan to me, so I'm always a little amazed how much it's served all around the tropical world. In many ways, it's a cold-weather dish ("cold weather" being a relative term). You're sure to see this coming out of bandanna-wearing cooks' kitchens whenever the temperature plunges way down close to 60.

Soak the beans overnight. In a large heavy saucepan, heat oil; brown the oxtail on all sides. Remove from the pan. Add the onion, carrots, celery, garlic and Scotch bonnet; sauté until caramelized. Return oxtail to the pan. Add stock, water and wine.

Drain the beans and add to the pot. Add thyme. Bring to a boil. Reduce heat; cover and simmer until oxtails are tender, 1 to 1¼ hours. Season with salt and pepper. Transfer oxtail pieces to plates; spoon beans and sauce over the top and alongside.

Serves 4

1 cup uncooked broad beans

¼ cup olive oil

2 pounds oxtail, cut at joints

1 yellow onion, finely chopped

2 carrots, finely chopped

1 rib celery, finely chopped

1 teaspoon minced garlic

1 Scotch bonnet pepper, seeded and chopped

4 cups Beef Stock (recipe on page 148)

½ cup water

¼ cup red wine

1 teaspoon fresh thyme leaves

Salt and freshly ground black pepper to taste

Culinary Origins
23° 7' N – 10° 38' N
82° 21' W – 61° 31' W

Ultimate Meat and Potatoes
Ultimate Meat and Potatoes

In Texas, beef brisket becomes barbecue. In my adopted home of New Orleans, it makes beef stock on the way to becoming "boiled brisket of beef." Here, however, we rethink the whole business, turning the beef into a fricassee and serving it with malanga purée instead of mashed potatoes, foie gras and quail eggs.

In a large pot, sear the brisket in oil on all sides. Add the celery, onions and carrots; cook and stir until caramelized. Stir in tomatoes and thyme, then add the stock. Bring to a boil. Reduce heat; cover and cook until meat is very tender, about 2 hours. Cool; shred and return meat to the broth. Heat through again before serving.

Cook malanga in boiling water until soft, about 15 minutes. Drain and purée with butter. Season with salt and pepper; set aside. In a very hot sauté pan, sear the foie gras quickly, 30 seconds on the first side and 15 seconds on the other. Remove foie gras and reduce heat to medium. Crack quail eggs into the remaining fat and cook sunny-side up.

To serve, place the shredded, brothy brisket in the bottom of a ring mold; top with a layer of malanga purée. Remove the mold; add seared foie gras, topped by the quail egg.

Serves 4

1 beef brisket (5 pounds)

2 tablespoons vegetable oil

5 ribs celery, chopped

2 yellow onions, chopped

4 carrots, chopped

8 tomatoes, chopped

1 teaspoon chopped fresh thyme

8 cups Chicken Stock
   (recipe on page 148)

2 pounds malanga, peeled and sliced

4 cups boiling water

1 tablespoon unsalted butter

Salt and freshly ground black pepper
   to taste

4 slices foie gras

4 quail eggs

Sensational Sides

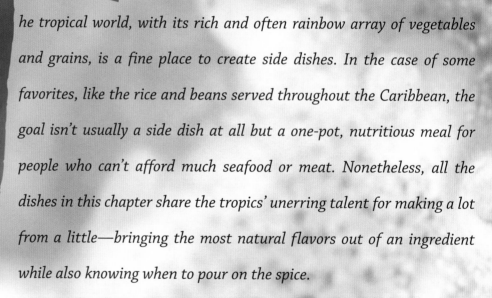

The tropical world, with its rich and often rainbow array of vegetables and grains, is a fine place to create side dishes. In the case of some favorites, like the rice and beans served throughout the Caribbean, the goal isn't usually a side dish at all but a one-pot, nutritious meal for people who can't afford much seafood or meat. Nonetheless, all the dishes in this chapter share the tropics' unerring talent for making a lot from a little—bringing the most natural flavors out of an ingredient while also knowing when to pour on the spice.

Included here are not only universal classics, like mashed potatoes and ratatouille, but foods from my childhood, such as Indian pickled vegetables and a chutney of tamarind and coconut. As with all the other chapters in this book, our approach to side dishes is "no borders" and "no limits." The results, as you'll see, can be very satisfying.

Garlic Mashed Potatoes

Garlic Mashed Potatoes

10 potatoes (preferably Yukon Gold)
2 cloves garlic, finely crushed
1 shallot, finely chopped
3 tablespoons butter
5 tablespoons heavy cream
Salt and black pepper to taste

In recent years, everyone has enjoyed discovering how much better garlic makes mashed potatoes. And when the potatoes are the smooth, flavorful and almost buttery Yukon Gold to start with, you know you're in for a treat.

Place potatoes in a large saucepan; cover with cold salted water. Bring to a boil. Reduce heat; simmer for 30 minutes or until tender. Meanwhile, in a small saucepan over medium heat, cook garlic and shallot in butter until soft; add cream. Keep warm. Drain potatoes and peel while still hot; blend in a mixing bowl until smooth. Stir in warm cream mixture. Season with salt and pepper.

Serves 8–10

Golden Potato Cakes

Golden Potato Cakes

6 medium potatoes, peeled and
   quartered
½ cup finely chopped red onion
¼ cup finely chopped green bell pepper
¼ cup finely chopped red bell pepper
1 Scotch bonnet pepper, seeded and
   minced
2 teaspoons plus 2 tablespoons olive
   oil, *divided*
½ teaspoon salt
¼ teaspoon black pepper

The plain white "Irish" potatoes most people in the West take for granted can still be something of a rarity in the islands. So the temptation is to stretch them and make them even more special by adding other ingredients.

Cook potatoes in lightly salted water for 20–25 minutes; drain. In a mixing bowl, mash the potatoes until smooth. In a skillet, sauté the onion, bell peppers and Scotch bonnet in 2 teaspoons oil until lightly caramelized. Add to the potato purée. Add salt and pepper; mix thoroughly.

   Divide the mixture into eight patties. Pan-fry in remaining oil until golden brown on both sides. Serve warm.

Serves 8

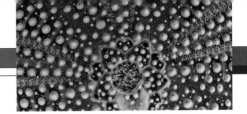

Saffron Couscous Cakes

Saffron Couscous Cakes

Couscous is a small grain usually associated with Morocco and the rest of North Africa. It has such a great texture, though, that chefs and home cooks have begun borrowing it for all sorts of meals. These cakes are a good example of the grain's versatility.

In a saucepan, bring cream to a boil; add saffron and boil for 1 minute. Add tomatoes and stock. Boil for 5 minutes. Transfer to a large mixing bowl. Add couscous. Fold in egg yolks; add ratatouille. Season with salt and pepper.

   Preheat oven to 300°. Transfer couscous mixture to a 13-inch x 9-inch x 2-inch inch baking pan. Bake for 25 minutes. Cool. Cut into cakes with a round cutter. When ready to serve, sauté in oil.

Serves 8

1 cup heavy cream

10 threads saffron

12 Roma tomatoes, chopped

5 cups Chicken Stock
(recipe on page 148)

2 cups uncooked couscous

3 egg yolks

Oven-Dried Tomato Ratatouille
(recipe below)

Sea salt and black pepper to taste

1 tablespoon olive oil

Oven-Dried Tomato Ratatouille

Oven-Dried Tomato Ratatouille

½ cup diced eggplant

½ cup olive oil

½ cup diced red onion

½ cup diced zucchini
(green part only)

½ cup diced yellow squash

½ cup diced green bell pepper

½ cup diced red bell pepper

½ cup diced yellow bell pepper

½ cup diced Oven-Dried Tomatoes
(recipe on page 31)

1 tablespoon minced garlic

As so often in my cooking, it's about going the extra mile. The Provençal dish ratatouille is often made with simple tomatoes, and it can taste fine that way. But there's no way to measure the extra nuances and flavor delivered by using oven-dried tomatoes.

In a large sauté pan, sauté eggplant in oil for 2 minutes. Add onion; sauté 1 minute longer. Add remaining ingredients; sauté for 3 minutes. Remove from the heat. Serve hot or at room temperature.

Serves 8

Aromatic Basmati Rice

Aromatic Basmati Rice

2 cups uncooked basmati rice
1½ tablespoons unsalted butter
1 tablespoon finely chopped shallots
3 cups water

Culinary Origins
18° 56′ N
72° 51′ E

For the longest time in America, rice was just plain rice. But first with imported rices like basmati from India, and finally with the growing of those varieties here, we've come to appreciate the different aromatics and textures of what had once seemed so simple.

Wash rice in a colander under running water for 1 minute; drain well. In a large pot, melt the butter; sauté shallots for 1 minute. Stir in the rice; cook for 1 minute. Add water. Cover and reduce heat to low. Cook for 15 minutes or until the liquid is absorbed.

Serves 4–6

Spiced Jasmine Rice

Spiced Jasmine Rice

2½ cups uncooked jasmine rice
1 teaspoon Homemade Garam
   Masala (recipe on page 140)
1 teaspoon ground turmeric
4 cups water
Salt and freshly ground black pepper
   to taste

Culinary Origins
13° 44′ N
100° 30′ E

Most people know jasmine rice as part of Thai and sometimes Vietnamese cuisine. In this case, though, it takes on a definite tint and taste of India.

In a mixing bowl, combine the rice, garam masala and turmeric. Transfer to a rice cooker; add the water, salt and pepper. Cook for 20 minutes or until fluffy.

   Or, to cook on the stovetop, combine all ingredients in a saucepan. Bring to a boil. Cover and reduce heat; simmer for 15 minutes or until all the liquid is absorbed. Remove from the heat; let stand for 10 minutes.

Serves 4–6

Classic Rice and Peas

Classic Rice and Peas

By many names, this is THE side dish of the Caribbean—the word "peas" being an affectionate island way of referring to almost every type and size of bean. In general, it's the survival of millions of poor people around the world—an affordable and amazing act of nutrition for one little plate. We love the smooth, rounded, slightly sweet taste that the coconut milk delivers.

1 cup dried red kidney beans *or* pigeon peas

2 cups Coconut Milk (recipe on page 147)

3 cups uncooked long-grain rice

2 cups water

1 tablespoon Worcestershire sauce

1 tablespoon sugar

2 green onions, finely chopped

1 sprig fresh thyme, finely chopped

2 teaspoons salt

1 teaspoon minced garlic

Soak the kidney beans in enough water to cover overnight. Drain and discard the water. Place beans in a large saucepan; add milk. Cook for 1 hour or until tender. Add the remaining ingredients. Cover and simmer for 20 minutes or until the rice is cooked and the liquid is absorbed (add a little more water if necessary).

Serves 10

Indian Pickled Vegetables

Indian Pickled Vegetables

Pickling Liquid

8 cups white vinegar

1½ cups coarse-ground mustard

2½ cups ground turmeric

2 cups chopped ginger

1 cup whole peppercorns

2 bunches cilantro, roughly chopped

10 jalapeño peppers, stems removed

5 cups vegetable oil

Vegetables

1 pound haricots verts (green beans), trimmed

5 large carrots, cut into matchsticks

1 head cauliflower, cut into florets

1 bunch broccoli, cut into florets

Culinary Origins

18° 56′ N
72° 51′ E

I think you'll love this bright yellow collection of pickled vegetables. Pickling time makes the flavors intensify, so you can experiment with both time and amounts to please you and your guests.

To prepare the pickling liquid, combine the first seven ingredients in a large bowl or container; cover and refrigerate for 1 week for flavors to develop. When ready to use, strain through cheesecloth and incorporate the oil.

Bring a large pot of water to a boil. Add the vegetables and blanch for 30 seconds. Cool quickly by placing vegetables in an ice-water bath; drain. Place vegetables on baking sheets; dry in the sun for 2 hours or place in a 180° oven for 30 minutes.

Using a clean spoon, transfer the vegetables to two sterilized mason jars. Pour pickling liquid over the top, making sure vegetables are covered. Seal jars and refrigerate for 3 weeks before serving. Can be stored for up to 6 months.

Serves 8–10

Tamarind Coconut Chutney

Tamarind Coconut Chutney

Tamarind is a tropical fruit we don't use much in the United States, but it's starting to turn up in many rich immigrant cultures, from Hispanic to West Indian to South Asian. You can make your own pulp or paste pretty easily, or it's increasingly for sale commercially as a shortcut.

In a blender, purée the tamarind, milk, oil, ginger juice, garlic and jalapeño. Add the coconut, cilantro and mint; blend until smoothly incorporated. Season with salt and pepper.

Makes about 5 cups

2 cups Tamarind Purée
  (recipe on page 146)
1 cup Coconut Milk
  (recipe on page 147)
3 tablespoons olive oil
1 teaspoon ginger juice
1 clove garlic, finely chopped
1 jalapeño pepper, stem removed
Meat of 1 coconut, grated
1 teaspoon chopped fresh cilantro
1 teaspoon chopped fresh mint
Salt and freshly ground black pepper
  to taste

Culinary Origins
20° 10' S
57° 30' E

107

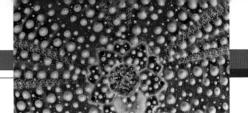

Mirlitons Au Gratin

Mirlitons Au Gratin

An amazing diversity of cultures love eating mirlitons—the French name that's still used for them in New Orleans. This gourdlike fruit also has an amazing variety of names that it's known by, among them chayote, vegetable pear and cho-cho.

Boil the whole mirlitons in a pot of salted water for 30 minutes or until tender; drain and cool. Cut each mirliton in half and scoop out pulp, leaving the shells intact. Mash the pulp; set aside. In a large skillet, heat 5 tablespoons butter; sauté onion and garlic until soft. Stir in the mirliton pulp, salt and pepper; cook 2 minutes longer. Remove from the heat; stir in 1½ cups Parmesan cheese.

   Preheat oven to 350°. Stuff filling into mirliton shells. Top each with 1 teaspoon remaining butter, the breadcrumbs and the remaining cheese. Place on a baking sheet. Bake for 15–20 minutes or until tops are golden brown.

Serves 6

3 large mirlitons

7 tablespoons butter, *divided*

2 cups chopped yellow onion

1 teaspoon minced garlic

1 teaspoon salt

1 teaspoon freshly ground black pepper

2 cups grated Parmesan cheese, *divided*

½ cup unseasoned breadcrumbs

Culinary Origins
29° 57′ N
90° 4′ W

A Rainbow of Desserts

Seen a certain way, dessert is the most tropical course anyone could ever imagine. How else could you respond to a set of recipes driven by a rainbow of fresh tropical fruits and powered, above all, by the ultimate product of the tropics, sugar? After that, though, things get a bit more tangled.

As with every other course, dessert in the tropics varies according to the ethnic mix of the island or region—Latin here, colonial European there, Asian somewhere else. When Christmas comes around and everyone on the islands of Barbados, Antigua and Jamaica starts making English plum pudding, you definitely know you're not in Kansas anymore. But you also know you're someplace very sweet and very special.

Mango and Coconut Soufflé Glacé

Mango and Coconut Soufflé Glacé

Here is one of the restaurant's most popular desserts—a complex construction that repays every ounce of effort with flavor. Since it's made in advance, it lets you enjoy your own dinner party.

Preheat oven to 350°. With a mixer, beat the eggs, sugar, vanilla and honey on high speed until mixture is about triple in volume, about 8 minutes. Add flour-cocoa mixture and incorporate with a whisk. Line a 9-inch square cake pan with parchment paper and coat with nonstick cooking spray.

Pour batter into pan. Bake for 15 minutes or until golden and a cake tester inserted in center comes out clean. Cool for 10 minutes; remove from pan to a wire rack to cool completely.

Soften gelatin in water. Meanwhile, in a stainless steel mixing bowl, whisk egg whites and confectioners' sugar over boiling water until meringue reaches 140° on a cooking thermometer and soft peaks form. Squeeze out excess water from gelatin and dissolve in meringue while still warm.

Whip the cream until soft peaks form. Place the mango and coconut purées in separate bowls; fold meringue into each purée, followed by whipped cream.

Pour mango mixture into a dessert mold; stir gently to remove air bubbles. Top with coconut mixture. Slice the cooled cake to fit over soufflé; place on top. Freeze for 6 hours.

To unmold, dip the bottom of the mold in hot water; turn out cake side down on a chilled dessert plate.

Serves 8–10

Génoise

6 eggs

⅓ cup sugar

1 teaspoon vanilla extract

1 teaspoon honey

⅓ cup all-purpose flour and baking cocoa combined

Soufflé

½ sheet unflavored gelatin

1 cup cool water

¾ cup egg whites

1¼ cups confectioners' sugar

2 cups heavy cream

½ cup mango purée

½ cup coconut purée

Culinary Origins
23° 7′ N – 10° 38′ N
82° 21′ W – 61° 31′ W

Lemongrass Panna Cotta
Lemongrass Panna Cotta

The Italian dessert panna cotta is so simple ... the name means nothing more than "cooked cream." But once we take it on a tour of tropical Asia, you'll forget a lot of the more mundane versions you've sampled elsewhere.

In a saucepan, combine the cream, milk, sugar, vanilla bean and lemongrass. Bring to a boil; remove from the heat. Let flavors infuse for 1 hour. Return to a boil. Soften the gelatin in water; stir into hot cream mixture until completely dissolved. Strain into a container with a pouring spout; pour into martini glasses. Refrigerate until set, 4–5 hours.

To make the filling, in a saucepan, heat half of the sugar with all of the lemon juice and butter until butter is melted. In a bowl, lightly beat the egg yolks with cornstarch and remaining sugar. Add to the butter mixture over heat, stirring continually until thickened. Transfer to a bowl; refrigerate until chilled.

Top panna cotta with passion fruit purée. Spoon the lemon filling into clean eggshells; serve alongside the panna cotta.

Serves 6

1 quart heavy cream
1½ cups whole milk
½ cup sugar
1 vanilla bean
2 to 3 stalks lemongrass
4 to 5 sheets unflavored gelatin
2 cups cool water
Lemon Filling
1¾ cups sugar, *divided*
¾ cup freshly squeezed lemon juice
½ cup plus 6 tablespoons unsalted butter
8 egg yolks
⅓ cup cornstarch
½ cup prepared passion fruit purée

Culinary Origins
13° 44′ N
100° 30′ E

Caramelized Pineapple Tarte Tatin

Caramelized Pineapple Tarte Tatin

Historically, the French tarte Tatin is made with apples, but it's an easy and totally delicious leap to make it with pineapple slices instead. This is more of a loving tribute to tarte Tatin anyway, since there's no actual pastry shell involved.

Crystallized Ginger Ice Cream

1 quart whole milk

⅓ quart heavy cream

1 large piece fresh ginger

12 egg yolks

1¼ cups sugar

¼ cup candied ginger pieces

Tarte Tatin

1 whole pineapple

2 cups pineapple juice

1 cup sugar

2 sticks (3 inches) cinnamon

1 large piece fresh ginger

4 allspice berries *or* ¼ teaspoon ground allspice

¼ cup confectioners' sugar

8 sheets brik leaves (thin Moroccan pastry)

¼ cup butter, melted

2¼ cups sugar, *divided*

In a saucepan, bring the milk, cream and fresh ginger to a boil. In a large mixing bowl, lightly beat egg yolks and sugar. Temper with a small amount of hot milk mixture, then stir in the rest until thoroughly incorporated. Return all to the saucepan; stir over low heat until thickened. Strain and chill. Stir in the candied ginger. Transfer to an ice cream maker, preparing according to manufacturer's instructions.

Core and cut the pineapple into eight 1-inch-thick slices from the middle, leaving the small end pieces for drying. Place the slices in a saucepan; add pineapple juice, sugar, cinnamon, ginger and allspice. Bring to a boil; remove from the heat. Let flavors infuse for 2 hours.

Meanwhile, carefully slice the remaining pineapple pieces paper-thin; dust both sides with confectioners' sugar. Place on a parchment paper-lined pan in a 200° oven for 30 minutes. Remove from pan while warm to prevent sticking. Cool on a clean, flat surface.

Increase oven temperature to 350°. Brush the brik leaves with butter and sprinkle with ¼ cup sugar. Cut each sheet into four squares; place on a silicon sheet coated with nonstick cooking spray. Bake just until golden, about 5 minutes. Cool on a wire rack.

Remove and discard ginger, cinnamon sticks and allspice berries from pineapple slice mixture; set caramelized pineapple aside. Transfer 1½ cups of the liquid to a saucepan; add remaining sugar. Bring to a boil; cook until reduced and thickened, 8–10 minutes. Keep syrup warm.

To serve, arrange four brik squares on a dessert plate; top with a caramelized pineapple slice. Scoop some crystallized ginger ice cream into the hole left by the core. Top with a slice of dried pineapple. Spoon syrup over dessert and around plate.

Serves 8

Cappamisu
Cappamisu

When tiramisu became all the rage in Italian restaurants, I found myself entertaining the simplest thought: What if we made it with cappuccino instead of espresso? And then … what if we made that cappuccino with the wonderful Blue Mountain coffee of Jamaica? The rest is dessert history!

Mocha Wafers
6 eggs, *separated*

½ cup brewed Blue Mountain coffee

½ cup baking cocoa

3 tablespoons corn syrup

4 cups sugar, *divided*

1 teaspoon salt

4 cups all-purpose flour

Pastry Cream
1 cup heavy cream

1 cup whole milk

½ cup sugar

1 tablespoon vanilla extract

1 tablespoon unflavored gelatin

2 tablespoons water

4 egg yolks

1 cup cornstarch

Coffee Cream
½ pound mascarpone cheese

2 cups heavy cream

½ cup brewed Blue Mountain coffee

1 tablespoon Kahlúa

1 tablespoon cognac *or* other brandy

1 teaspoon ground allspice

Kahlúa Coffee
¼ cup brewed Blue Mountain coffee

2 tablespoons heavy cream

2 tablespoons Kahlúa

Preheat oven to 350°. With a mixer, mix the egg yolks, coffee, cocoa and corn syrup until smooth. Whip in 2 cups sugar. In a large stainless steel bowl, whip the egg whites and salt until soft peaks form. Add remaining sugar. Fold in the egg yolk mixture. Sift in flour, 1 cup at a time, until smooth.

Drop dough by heaping tablespoonfuls onto a greased baking sheet. Bake for 10 minutes. Cool on a wire rack.

To make the pastry cream, heat the cream, milk, sugar and vanilla in a small saucepan until mixture comes to a simmer. In a bowl, soften gelatin in water; add egg yolks and cornstarch. Slowly add hot cream mixture, stirring until smooth. Refrigerate for 3 hours.

Place 1 cup pastry cream in a mixing bowl. (Save the leftover pastry cream for icing cakes or filling profiteroles or éclairs.) Add the remaining coffee cream ingredients; whip until blended. In a small bowl, stir together the Kahlúa coffee ingredients.

To assemble, fill a pastry bag with coffee cream; pipe enough into 10 glass coffee cups to be about one-third full. Top each with a mocha wafer, then pour about 1 tablespoon of Kahlúa coffee on each wafer. Fill the cup the rest of the way with coffee cream; smooth the top with a spatula. Refrigerate for 1 hour before serving.

Serves 10

Floating Island with Crème Anglaise

Floating Island with Crème Anglaise

8 egg yolks

¾ cup sugar, *divided*

1 quart half-and-half cream

2 vanilla beans, *divided*

1½ cups egg whites

4⅔ cups confectioners' sugar

2 quarts whole milk

Really nothing more than a type of meringue, floating island (the English name for the French "oeuf a la niege") is a classic dessert we think is overdue for rediscovery. It's one of those dishes that came to the tropics with the colonial powers, in this case France and England, and it remains popular on their respectively influenced islands.

To prepare the crème anglaise, in a mixer, lightly beat egg yolks and ¼ cup sugar. In a saucepan, bring half-and-half to a boil. Remove from the heat. Scrape the seeds from one vanilla bean into the cream, then add the pod. Temper yolk mixture with a small amount of hot cream, then stir in the rest. Let stand for 1 minute. Strain into a chilled bowl. Refrigerate for at least 30 minutes, stirring every 5 minutes.

For meringue, mix the egg whites and confectioners' sugar in a bowl. Place over a pot of boiling water and stir until a cooking thermometer registers 140°. With a mixer, beat on high speed for 10 minutes.

In a separate saucepan, combine the milk, remaining sugar and remaining vanilla bean. Bring to a boil; remove from the heat. Immediately place ice-cream scoopfuls of meringue into the hot milk mixture. Let stand for 5 minutes; turn and let stand 5 minutes longer. With a slotted spoon, remove meringue balls and place on a parchment paper-lined baking pan. Cover and refrigerate. Discard poaching liquid.

To serve, fill a martini glass two-thirds to the top with crème anglaise; set a meringue "island" on top.

Serves 10–12

Chocolate-Glazed Papaya Cake

Chocolate-Glazed Papaya Cake

The idea of a "fruit cake" may not be your cup of tea, but that's only because you're thinking of that gift that keeps on giving during the holidays. This rich, moist cake with chocolate glaze should prove powerful enough to turn your opinion around.

Preheat oven to 350°. Butter and flour a large springform pan. With a mixer, blend the butter, brown sugar and honey. Beat in eggs, one at a time. Thoroughly incorporate the papaya purée. Sift together the flour, baking soda, cinnamon, salt, allspice and nutmeg; slowly blend into papaya mixture.

Pour into prepared pan. Bake for 35–40 minutes or until a cake tester inserted in the center comes out clean. Turn cake out onto a wire rack and cool completely.

In a saucepan, melt the chocolate with sugar and cream, stirring to prevent burning. Pour warm glaze over cooled cake, making certain it covers the sides. Refrigerate for at least 20 minutes. To serve, decorate with sliced papaya and whipped cream.

Serves 10

1½ cups unsalted butter, softened
½ cup packed brown sugar
⅓ cup honey
2 eggs
2 cups fresh papaya purée
3 cups all-purpose flour
2 teaspoons baking soda
1 teaspoon ground cinnamon
½ teaspoon salt
½ teaspoon ground allspice
½ teaspoon freshly ground nutmeg
1½ pounds semisweet chocolate, chopped
¼ cup sugar
1 cup heavy cream
Sliced papaya and whipped cream for garnish

Culinary Origins
23° 7′ N – 10° 38′ N
82° 21′ W – 61° 31′ W

Chocolate Soufflés

Chocolate Soufflés

Even though it's considered an old-fashioned dessert, there's nothing quite like the pleasure you get from a warm chocolate soufflé served right out of the oven. We serve them every night at the restaurant, and people still act like we've worked some kind of miracle. It's no miracle, though. Just follow these time-tested steps, and you can seem to be a "miracle worker" too.

This first step must be completed 24 hours before serving. In the top of a double boiler, melt butter; stir in chocolate chips until melted and incorporated. Remove from the heat. In a mixer with the whisk attachment, beat the eggs and sugar until doubled in volume, about 5 minutes. Add cornstarch, beating until smooth. Pour into the chocolate mixture; whisk until smooth. Transfer to a bowl or storage container. Cover and refrigerate overnight.

When ready to bake, preheat oven to 350°. Line the sides of eight 3-inch metal rings with parchment paper and cut out paper circles to cover the ring bottoms on a baking sheet; coat the paper with nonstick cooking spray. Spoon about ³/₄ cup of soufflé batter into each prepared ring. Bake for 30 minutes.

Meanwhile, in a saucepan, combine the water, sugar, cocoa, cream, vanilla and chocolate chips. Cook and stir over medium heat until sauce comes to a boil. Remove from the heat; cool.

To serve, gently unmold each soufflé by removing the bottom paper, then lifting off the ring and peeling the paper from the sides. Transfer soufflés to dessert plates; lightly dust with confectioners' sugar and spoon chocolate sauce on top.

Serves 8

1 cup plus 2 tablespoons unsalted butter
2 cups bittersweet chocolate chips
5 eggs
1½ cups sugar
¼ cup cornstarch
Chocolate Sauce
1 cup water
1½ cups sugar
1 cup baking cocoa
½ cup heavy cream
1 teaspoon vanilla extract
¼ cup bittersweet chocolate chips
Confectioners' sugar for garnish

West African Sweet Potato Pie

West African Sweet Potato Pie

Crust

⅓ cup plus 1 tablespoon vegetable
   shortening

1 cup all-purpose flour

½ teaspoon salt

2 to 3 tablespoons cold water

Additional flour for dusting

Filling

2 cups mashed cooked sweet potatoes

2 eggs, beaten

1 tablespoon unsalted butter, softened

1 cup evaporated milk

¾ cup packed light brown sugar

½ cup light corn syrup

1 teaspoon vanilla extract

½ teaspoon ground ginger

½ teaspoon ground cinnamon

½ teaspoon freshly grated nutmeg

¼ teaspoon salt

Whipped cream

Never underestimate the contribution of African slaves to tropical cuisine, specifically that of the Caribbean that slowly made its way onto the plantations of the Old South. In a sense, so much of what little restaurants in the North serve as "soul food" today began its life as "tropical cuisine" a couple thousand miles to the south. Sweet potatoes came to the Americas from Africa with the slaves.

In a bowl, combine the shortening, flour and salt with a pastry cutter or your fingers. Add just enough water to form a dough. Gather into a ball; dust lightly with more flour. Cover with plastic wrap and refrigerate for 30 minutes.

On a floured work surface, roll the chilled dough into an 11-inch circle. Carefully transfer to a 9-inch pie plate and crimp the edge.

Preheat oven to 375°. In a mixing bowl, beat the sweet potatoes, eggs and butter. Mix in the milk, brown sugar, corn syrup, vanilla, ginger, cinnamon, nutmeg and salt. Pour into crust. Bake for 40–45 minutes or until set. Cool on a wire rack.

To serve, slice pie into wedges; place on dessert plates. Decorate with whipped cream.

Serves 8

Culinary Origins

14° 38' N

17° 27' W

Banana Fritters with Coffee-Rum Sauce

Banana Fritters with Coffee-Rum Sauce

In the islands, once the Spanish taught people to fry, nobody ever quite stopped ... and that means fritters abound. Day to day, you see mostly conch fritters and saltfish fritters. But when dessert time rolls around, we think you'll embrace these puffy banana confections with their glorious sauce balancing island coffee and island rum.

In a small saucepan, melt 1 cup sugar; add hot coffee, stirring constantly. Dissolve the cornstarch in cold coffee; stir into sugar mixture. Bring to a boil to thicken; remove from the heat. Incorporate the butter and rum. Keep sauce warm.

To make the fritters, sift together the flour, baking powder, salt and remaining sugar. Combine the egg, milk and shortening; stir into flour mixture until smooth. Slice each banana into 3–4 pieces; roll each piece in flour, then cover with batter.

Preheat oil to 375°. Fry the fritters in batches until golden on all sides, about 5 minutes. Drain on paper towels. Place on dessert plates; pour coffee-rum sauce over the fritters.

Serves 4

1¼ cups sugar, *divided*

1½ cups hot brewed coffee

2 tablespoons cornstarch

3 tablespoons cold brewed coffee

2 tablespoons unsalted butter

2 tablespoons dark rum

1 cup all-purpose flour

2 tablespoons baking powder

1¼ teaspoons salt

1 egg, well beaten

⅓ cup milk

2 teaspoons melted vegetable shortening

2 to 3 firm bananas

Additional flour for coating

Vegetable *or* peanut oil for deep-frying

Culinary Origins
23° 7′ N – 10° 38′ N
82° 21′ W – 61° 31′ W

Piña Colada Rice Pudding

Piña Colada Rice Pudding

2 cups cooked rice

2 cups milk, *divided*

1 cup coconut cream (like Coco Lopez)

¼ cup plus 2 tablespoons sugar, *divided*

4 tablespoons unsalted butter, *divided*

½ teaspoon salt

3 eggs, *separated*

2 cups crushed fresh pineapple

1½ teaspoons vanilla extract, *divided*

½ cup flaked unsweetened coconut

1 tablespoon cornstarch

½ cup freshly squeezed pineapple juice

¼ cup packed brown sugar

Culinary Origins
18° 29' N
66° 8' W

Even the simplest rice pudding—a bit of cooked rice, a splash of milk, a little sugar and a dusting of ground cinnamon—can be the perfect dessert on a hot summer day. We definitely take rice pudding to the next level here, adding the flavors of one of our favorite tropical drinks and then baking the whole wonderful thing in the oven.

In a 2-quart saucepan, combine the rice, 1½ cups milk, coconut cream, ¼ cup sugar, 1 tablespoon butter and salt. Cook until thick and creamy, about 15 minutes, stirring occasionally. Beat egg yolks with remaining milk; add to rice mixture and cook for 1 minute. Remove from the heat. Stir in pineapple and 1 teaspoon vanilla. Cool.

Preheat oven to 325°. In a mixer, beat egg whites and remaining sugar until peaks are stiff but not dry. Fold into the cooled rice mixture. Turn into six buttered ramekins. Sprinkle with coconut. Bake for 20–25 minutes or until tips of coconut start to turn golden.

In a saucepan, dissolve cornstarch in pineapple juice. Add brown sugar, remaining butter and an additional pinch of salt. Cook until clear and thickened, stirring frequently. Remove from the heat; add remaining vanilla. Spoon warm sauce over rice pudding.

Serves 6

Key Lime Crème Brûlée

Key Lime Crème Brûlée

I have long wanted to try combining two of the world's most popular desserts—Key lime pie and crème brûlée. There's never been any law against it, of course. It's just that some wonderful ideas take us a while to get around to. You should find this one worth the wait.

Preheat oven to 250°. With a mixer, beat egg yolks and sugar on medium speed. In a saucepan, bring cream to a boil; add to yolk mixture, beating constantly. Stir in the lime juice, vanilla and orange zest. Continue to beat until mixture is cool.

Pour into six ramekins. Place in a large baking pan; add water to the pan until it reaches halfway up the side of the ramekins. Bake for 50 minutes. Remove ramekins from pan; cool to room temperature. Refrigerate until chilled.

Just before serving, top each custard with brown sugar. Use a small torch or place the ramekins under a preheated broiler to cause the brown sugar to get crispy and caramelized (don't allow the sugar to burn).

6 egg yolks

⅓ cup sugar

2½ cups heavy cream

2 tablespoons freshly squeezed Key lime juice

1 tablespoon vanilla extract

1 teaspoon orange zest

3 tablespoons dark brown sugar

Serves 6

Culinary Origins
24° 33′ N
81° 46′ W

Flambéed Pineapple

Flambéed Pineapple

You could conceivably make this very simple dessert with canned pineapple chunks, but there's nothing to compare with the explosive sweetness of fresh chunks carved from the whole. For simplicity's sake, cut slices of whole pineapple crosswise, then trim off the rind. The rest is easy.

In a sauté pan, melt the butter; stir in brown sugar. Sauté the pineapple cubes until lightly caramelized and golden flecks appear on all sides. Carefully pour rum into the pan and flame. When the fire dies down, spoon the pineapple and sauce over ice cream in bowls.

3 tablespoons unsalted butter

3 tablespoons brown sugar

2 cups fresh pineapple cubes

¼ cup gold rum

Vanilla ice cream

Serves 4

Tropical Drinks

hether you're more like Errol Flynn downing gin on the dock for breakfast in Jamaica, or Somerset Maugham sipping a Singapore Sling on the hushed veranda of the Raffles Hotel, the tropics do have a tradition of plying us with great cocktails. In recent years, the popular imagination has tied these legacies to two separate strands of spirits: tequila in some of the Latin world and rum in the Caribbean. Yes, we like margaritas as much as the next person; but to us, a truly tropical drink is one made with rum.

Hopefully, you'll find among this brief collection from the thousands of recipes out there something as simple as the rediscovered mojito ... and something as complex as those colorful fruit-juice concoctions that are the chief memory of nearly every island vacation.

Yellow Bird

Yellow Bird

¾ cup orange juice

6 ounces Galliano

2 ounces rum

2 tablespoons freshly squeezed lime juice

½ ounce Tia Maria

½ ounce crème de banana

4 teaspoons sugar

4 ice cubes

Place all ingredients in a blender; blend until smooth. Pour into a 12-ounce Collins glass; garnish with tropical fruit.

Serves 1

Passion Fruit Daiquiri

Passion Fruit Daiquiri

¼ cup passion fruit juice

¼ cup freshly squeezed lime juice

2 ounces gold rum

2 cups crushed ice

Place all ingredients in a blender; blend at high speed until slushy. Pour into chilled glasses.

Serves 2

Caipirinha

Caipirinha

2 teaspoons sugar

8 lime wedges

Ice cubes

2½ ounces cachaça

In an old fashioned glass, muddle the sugar into the limes. Fill the glass with ice and add the cachaça; stir well.

Serves 1

Simple Syrup

1 cup water
1 cup sugar

In a heavy saucepan, bring water and sugar to a boil; stir until the sugar is dissolved. Cool and refrigerate.

Makes about 1 cup

Island Sky

2 ounces gold rum
¼ cup freshly squeezed lime juice
¼ cup Simple Syrup (recipe above)
1½ ounces blue curaçao
2 slices pineapple
2 cups crushed ice

Place all ingredients in a blender; blend at high speed until slushy. Pour into chilled glasses.

Serves 2

Classic Cuban Mojito

2 fresh mint leaves
2 lime wedges
¼ cup Simple Syrup (recipe above)
2 ounces white rum
1 cup crushed ice
2 tablespoons soda water
2 tablespoons ginger ale

Muddle the mint, lime and syrup; transfer to a cocktail shaker. Add rum and ice; shake well. Strain into a chilled glass; top with soda water and ginger ale.

Serves 1

Pink Lady

½ cup evaporated milk
¼ cup strawberry syrup
2 ounces white rum
4 ice cubes

Place all ingredients in a blender; blend until smooth. Strain into chilled glasses.

Serves 2

Mai Tai

1 ounce white rum
1 ounce dark rum
1 ounce orange curaçao *or* Grand Marnier
2 tablespoons orange juice
2 tablespoons pineapple juice
2 tablespoons freshly squeezed lime juice
½ ounce amaretto
½ ounce grenadine

Place all ingredients in a cocktail shaker; shake well. Pour into a glass filled with ice. Don't forget a paper umbrella for garnish!

Serves 1

Piña Colada

½ cup coconut cream (like Coco Lopez)
½ cup pineapple juice
1 ounce white rum
2 tablespoons half-and-half cream
1 cup crushed ice

Place all ingredients in a blender; blend until smooth. Pour into a chilled glass; garnish with tropical fruit.

Serves 1

Original Daiquiri

1½ ounces white rum

2 tablespoons freshly squeezed lime juice

1 teaspoon sugar

1 cup crushed ice

Place all ingredients in a cocktail shaker; shake well. Strain into a chilled glass.

Serves 1

Blue Hawaii

3 tablespoons coconut cream (like Coco Lopez)

3 tablespoons pineapple juice

1 ounce white rum

1 ounce blue curaçao

1 cup crushed ice

Place all ingredients in a blender; blend until smooth. Pour into a chilled glass; garnish with tropical fruit.

Serves 1

Mango Margarita

6 tablespoons sour mix

1¼ ounces premium tequila

¾ ounce Grand Marnier

1½ tablespoons fresh mango purée

½ cup crushed ice

Salt

1 lime slice

Place the first five ingredients in a cocktail shaker; shake well. Pour into a chilled glass rimmed with salt; garnish with lime.

Serves 1

Planter's Punch

Planter's Punch

2 ounces white rum
2 tablespoons sugar
2 tablespoons water
½ tablespoon freshly squeezed lime juice
1 pineapple slice, chopped
Crushed ice
1 maraschino cherry

Stir the rum, sugar, water and lime juice until sugar is dissolved; add pineapple. Pour into a glass filled with ice; garnish with a cherry.

Serves 1

Rum Collins

Rum Collins

4 ounces white rum
2 tablespoons freshly squeezed lime juice
2 tablespoons sugar
Crushed ice
Soda water
1 lime slice

Stir the rum, lime juice and sugar until sugar is dissolved. Pour into a tall glass filled with ice; add a splash of soda water. Garnish with lime.

Serves 1

Reggae Sunsplash

Reggae Sunsplash

¼ cup pineapple juice
2 tablespoons freshly squeezed lime juice
2 tablespoons strawberry syrup
1 ounce gold rum
½ ounce Yellow Chartreuse
Crushed ice

Combine the first five ingredients; pour into a tall glass filled with ice.

Serves 1

Island Coffee

4 cups hot brewed coffee
1¼ cups thinly sliced orange peel
1 orange, peeled and sliced
1 tablespoon sugar
1 teaspoon aromatic bitters
½ cup whipped cream

Measure the coffee into a flameproof pot over heat; add the orange peel and slices. Steep for 15 minutes. Add the sugar and bitters. Strain into warmed heatproof glasses; top with whipped cream.

Serves 6

Nonalcoholic Tropical Punch

¼ cup pineapple juice
¼ cup orange juice
¼ cup apple juice
¼ cup mango nectar
¼ cup strawberry syrup
1 cup ice cubes

Place all ingredients in a cocktail shaker; shake well. Pour into chilled glasses.

Serves 2

Back to the Basics

Good cooking, whatever your personal style in the kitchen, always involves some type of basics. You might be a simple backyard griller, for instance, but that probably means you have a secret spice mix, dry rub or liquid marinade that makes a beef brisket or slab of pork ribs feel like your own. In the professional chef's kitchen, naturally, these basics take on tremendous importance—not only as a cook's signature flavors, but as the key to consistency that customers demand.

What follows is a collection of foundational items, limited by nothing and no one, that do indeed unlock the door to a new style of global tropical cooking. At the end of this chapter, you'll find recipes for some of the most commonly used stocks … they stand ready to deliver intense flavors whenever you add them to a dish, whether one from this book or one of your own creation.

Homemade Garam Masala

Homemade Garam Masala

10 cups coriander seeds

3 cups mixed peppercorns

3 cups green cardamom seeds

2½ cups cumin seeds

8 sticks (3 inches) cinnamon

1 cup ground nutmeg

20 bay leaves

In a large sauté pan over medium heat, toast the coriander, peppercorns, cardamom, cumin and cinnamon for 3 minutes. Remove from the heat; cool. Add nutmeg and bay leaves; grind in a coffee mill. Store in an airtight container in the refrigerator for up to 3 months.

Homemade Curry Powder

Homemade Curry Powder

3½ cups green cardamom seeds

3 cups cumin seeds

1 cup plus 2 tablespoons mixed peppercorns

2¼ cups coriander seeds

⅔ cup whole cloves

2½ cups ground turmeric

¾ cup paprika

½ cup ground red pepper

In a large sauté pan over medium heat, toast the cardamom, cumin, peppercorns, coriander and cloves for 3 minutes. Remove from the heat; cool. Add turmeric, paprika and red pepper; grind in a coffee mill. Store in an airtight container in the refrigerator for up to 3 months.

Jerk Marinade

2 cups vegetable oil

2 large onions, chopped

10 cloves garlic

6 scallions

1 Scotch bonnet pepper, seeded

2 bay leaves

1 tablespoon minced fresh thyme

1 teaspoon freshly ground allspice

1 teaspoon black pepper

1 teaspoon sea salt

½ teaspoon freshly ground coriander

½ cup dark rum

Juice of 2 limes

In a large sauté pan, heat oil. Add the onions, garlic and scallions; cook for 5 minutes or until lightly caramelized. Add the Scotch bonnet, bay leaves, thyme, allspice, pepper, salt and coriander; cook 3 minutes longer. Add the rum and lime juice; cook until the liquid is mostly evaporated. Cool; purée in a food processor. Store in the refrigerator for up to 3 weeks.

Peri-Peri Sauce

3 yellow onions, chopped

3 cloves garlic

¼ cup vegetable *or* olive oil

2 Pickled Lemons (recipe on page 143)

3 jalapeño peppers, seeded

1 cup ground peri-peri *or* chimayo pepper

1 tablespoon freshly ground cumin

1 tablespoon freshly ground coriander

½ teaspoon sea salt

3 cups olive oil

In a large sauté pan, sauté onions and garlic in ¼ cup oil until lightly browned. Remove from the heat; cool. Transfer to a food processor; add the lemons, jalapeños, peri-peri, cumin, coriander and salt; purée. Emulsify with the olive oil. Store in the refrigerator for up to 3 weeks.

Indian Vindaye

Indian Vindaye

You can make your own garam masala or curry powder for this pickling liquid; see the recipes on page 140. This is best made the day before using.

½ cup finely diced ginger

2 tablespoons minced garlic

2 yellow onions, finely diced

4 cups vegetable oil, *divided*

2 tablespoons ground turmeric

1 tablespoon garam masala *or* curry powder

2 jalapeño peppers, seeded and diced

1 teaspoon sea salt

1 teaspoon freshly ground black pepper

1 cup white wine vinegar

2 tablespoons whole-grain mustard

In a saucepan over medium heat, sauté the ginger, garlic and onions in 1 cup oil for 3 minutes. Add turmeric, garam masala, jalapeños, salt and pepper; cook for 2 minutes. Stir in the vinegar, mustard and remaining oil. Remove from the heat. Transfer to a bowl; cover and refrigerate.

Pickled Green Mangoes

Pickled Green Mangoes

This recipe should be prepared at least 2 weeks before serving.

10 unripe mangoes

Fleur de Sel

3 tablespoons mustard seeds

1 tablespoon coriander seeds

4 tablespoons ground turmeric

2 tablespoons red pepper flakes

10 cloves garlic, minced

6 cups vegetable oil

3 jalapeño peppers, seeded and quartered

Wash and peel the mangoes. Remove the seeds, cut the flesh into four pieces and split them in half. Place on parchment paper; sprinkle with fleur de sel. Leave in the sun for 4 hours, turning occasionally.

Using a mortar and pestle, crush the mustard and coriander seeds. Add turmeric, pepper flakes and garlic. Mix with oil. Place mangoes in jars; add jalapeños. Pour oil mixture over the top (mangoes need to be submerged in oil); seal jars. Leave where there is plenty of sunlight for 2 days, then refrigerate for 2 weeks before using. This will keep for up to 6 months.

Pickled Lemons

Pickled Lemons

6 cups white wine

1 cup white wine vinegar

3 cups sugar

3 sprigs fresh thyme

3 tablespoons sea salt

1 tablespoon crushed red pepper

1 tablespoon ground turmeric

1 teaspoon mustard seeds

1 teaspoon black pepper

10 lemons, spiked with a fork

In a large saucepan, combine the first nine ingredients. Bring to a rolling boil. Add lemons. Reduce heat to low; simmer for 1 hour. Remove from the heat; steep until cool.

Place lemons in jars. Strain liquid and pour over lemons; seal jars. Store in a cool place. This is best made 2 weeks before using.

Harissa

Harissa

6 tablespoons olive oil
2 tablespoons minced garlic
½ cup diced leeks
½ cup diced celery
½ cup diced shallots
½ cup diced carrots
2 jalapeño peppers, seeded and diced
½ teaspoon coriander seeds
½ teaspoon finely chopped fresh mint

½ teaspoon caraway seeds
½ teaspoon sea salt
½ teaspoon freshly ground black pepper

In a large sauté pan, heat oil. Sauté the garlic, leeks, celery, shallots, carrots and jalapeños for 5–7 minutes or until golden brown. Cool; purée in a food processor. Mix in the coriander, mint, caraway, salt and pepper. Transfer to a glass bowl; refrigerate for 1 hour.

Chimichurri

Chimichurri

(See Variations at Right)

2 cups fresh parsley leaves
8 cloves garlic
1½ cups olive oil (preferably Spanish)
Juice of 2 lemons
1 tablespoon red pepper flakes
1 teaspoon sea salt
½ teaspoon black pepper

In a food processor, chop the parsley and garlic. Mix in the remaining ingredients. Let stand for 2 hours.

For Oven-Dried Tomato Chimichurri: Add 10 Oven-Dried Tomatoes (recipe on page 31), finely diced.

For Lemon Mustard Chimichurri: Add 1 cup finely diced Pickled Lemon (recipe on page 143) and 1 tablespoon ground mustard.

For Roasted Tomatillo Chimichurri: In a food processor, combine 10 tomatillos, ¼ cup olive oil, 2 cloves garlic, 1 jalapeño pepper and ¼ cup chopped onion; process until puréed. In a sauté pan over medium heat, sauté tomatillo purée for 5 minutes or until lightly colored. Finish in a 350° oven for 10 minutes. Cool; purée again. Add to original recipe.

Grapefruit and Scotch Bonnet Mojo
Grapefruit and Scotch Bonnet Mojo

2 cups grapeseed oil, *divided*

10 cloves garlic

1 cup freshly squeezed grapefruit juice

1 cup freshly squeezed lime juice

1 Scotch bonnet pepper, seeded and chopped

½ teaspoon ground coriander

½ teaspoon ground cumin

2 mint leaves

5 basil leaves

1 teaspoon sea salt

¼ teaspoon freshly ground black pepper

In a saucepan, heat ½ cup oil. Add garlic; cook until lightly toasted on all sides, about 1–2 minutes. Deglaze pan with grapefruit and lime juices. Bring to a rapid boil. Add the Scotch bonnet, coriander and cumin. Remove from the heat; cool.

Transfer to a blender; add mint, basil, salt and pepper. Emulsify with the remaining oil. Refrigerate. Emulsify again when ready to use.

Sauce Raita
Sauce Raita

2 cups plain yogurt

1 tablespoon Homemade Garam Masala
  (recipe on page 140)

1 tablespoon ground chimayo pepper

Juice of 2 lemons

3 cucumbers, peeled and finely chopped

2 green apples, peeled and finely chopped

2 tomatoes, peeled and finely chopped

10 fresh chives, finely chopped

¼ cup chopped fresh cilantro

Salt and freshly ground black pepper to taste

In a large bowl, combine the yogurt with garam masala and chimayo pepper. Stir in the lemon juice, cucumbers, apples, tomatoes, chives and cilantro. Season with salt and pepper. Chill.

Tamarind Purée

Tamarind Purée

2 pounds tamarind pods
4 cups hot water

Shell the pods; soak in hot water for 5 minutes. Pass through a sieve, pressing well to extract all of the pulp. Store in the refrigerator.

Coconut Milk

Coconut Milk

1 fresh coconut
Water

Crack the coconut and drain the liquid (called "coconut water" in the tropics) into a measuring cup. Add enough additional water to measure ½ cup.

Chop the white coconut meat and combine with this liquid in a blender or food processor to make a smooth purée. Pour into a saucepan; heat gently, letting the mixture steep for 30 minutes. Strain through cheesecloth. Store in the refrigerator for up to 1 week.

Homemade Mayonnaise

Homemade Mayonnaise

2 tablespoons red wine vinegar
2 tablespoons Dijon mustard
2 egg yolks
1½ cups olive oil
Salt (preferably kosher) and black pepper to taste

In a mixing bowl, combine the vinegar, mustard and egg yolks. Slowly whisk in oil until mixture is thoroughly incorporated. Season with salt and pepper. Store in the refrigerator for up to 3 days.

Chicken Stock

Chicken Stock

(See Variations at Right)

2 tablespoons vegetable oil
3 yellow onions, chopped
2 carrots, chopped
6 ribs celery, chopped
10 pounds chicken bones*
4 quarts cold water

In a large stockpot, heat oil over medium heat; sauté onions, carrots and celery for 3 minutes. Add chicken bones and cold water. Reduce heat; simmer for 3 hours. Skim fat and impurities as they rise to the top. Strain and reduce to 1 quart. Transfer to a storage container. Refrigerate for 4–5 days or freeze.

*For Beef Stock, Duck Stock or Veal Stock: Substitute 10 pounds of the appropriate meat bones; first brown in a 350° oven for 30–40 minutes before adding to the vegetables and water.

Crawfish Stock

Crawfish Stock

(See Variation at Right)

¼ cup olive oil
6 carrots, chopped
4 yellow onions, chopped
1 rib celery, chopped
2 leeks, chopped
5 pounds live crawfish*
4 cloves garlic
10 Oven-Dried Tomatoes (recipe on page 31)
1 gallon chicken stock *or* water
3 bay leaves

In a large stockpot, heat oil; sauté the carrots, onions, celery and leeks until lightly caramelized. Add crawfish and garlic. Stir in the tomatoes. Add stock and bay leaves. Bring to a boil for 20 minutes. Skim fat and impurities as they rise to the top. Transfer to a blender and blend thoroughly. Strain into a storage container. Refrigerate for 4–5 days or freeze.

*For Crab Stock: Substitute 5 pounds whole blue crabs for the crawfish.

Shrimp Stock

Shrimp Stock

2 tablespoons olive oil

6 carrots, chopped

4 yellow onions, chopped

1 rib celery, chopped

1 gallon chicken stock *or* water

3 bay leaves

5 pounds shrimp heads

In a large stockpot, heat oil; sauté the carrots, onions and celery until lightly caramelized. Add stock. Bring to a boil. Add bay leaves and shrimp heads. Return to a boil for 15 minutes. Skim fat and impurities as they rise to the top. Transfer to a blender and blend thoroughly. Strain into a storage container. Refrigerate for 4–5 days or freeze.

Lobster Stock

Lobster Stock

¾ cup olive, *divided*

5 pounds lobster torsos

6 carrots, chopped

4 yellow onions, chopped

2 ribs celery, chopped

2 leeks, chopped

2 cups dry sherry

1 cup Oven-Dried Tomatoes (recipe on page 31)

1 gallon chicken stock *or* water

4 Kaffir lime leaves

1 bunch parsley

Spread ¼ cup oil over the bottom of a large roasting pan. Layer lobster torsos in the pan. Roast at 350° for 15 minutes. Remove lobsters and set aside. Place the roasting pan on a burner over medium heat; heat the remaining oil. Add carrots, onions, celery and leeks; cook and stir for 10 minutes or until lightly caramelized. Deglaze the pan with sherry and stir to incorporate. Add tomatoes and stir to blend.

Transfer to a large stockpot; add the roasted lobster torsos, stock, lime leaves and parsley. Bring to a rolling boil for 20 minutes. Reduce heat; simmer for 15 minutes. Strain into a storage container. Refrigerate for 4–5 days or freeze.

Tropical Ingredients

Dominique's Glossary

For purposes of this book, tropical ingredients don't simply come from the Caribbean or from Latin America or Southeast Asia. Indeed, each region can and often does claim many of the same ingredients as their own, pointing with pride to a unique name given to a fruit, vegetable, herb or spice that may not be entirely unique.

What follows is our own look at the ingredients that make tropical cooking possible, recognizing as necessary when the same ingredient is known by different names in different tropical cultures.

Were we writing this 15 or 20 years ago, we would have gone out of our way to list mail-order sources or pointed with some uncertainty toward open markets in parts of your city you've probably never visited before. The amazing good news today is that nearly all tropical ingredients are available in many everyday supermarkets.

Plus, many ingredients that required expensive importation from exotic ports are now grown in the applicable sections of the United States—at the southern tip of Florida, for instance. Still others are grown in Mexico and shipped north across the border in sealed containers inspected and approved by our own USDA.

In other words, "exotic foods" don't have to be quite so exotic anymore. This is a wonderful leap forward for all of us who appreciate the adventure of tropical cookery.

Achiote: Popular by this name in Latin American cooking, and known as annatto to Caribbean cooks, these small dried seeds are used primarily for the bright yellow color they impart to anything they touch: Butter and some cheeses get color from the seeds themselves, but in Latin cooking, achiote turns up most often as an oil that's been tinted by frying the seeds. Paella, roasted chicken, soups and stews all get a yellow-orange hue from time spent in the company of achiote. Saffron or turmeric can be substituted, reflecting their use in India and other spice-loving South Asian cultures.

Ackee: The infamous Captain Bligh introduced ackee to the Caribbean from West Africa, though for the most part only Jamaica embraced the fruit as being edible. With the increasing embrace of things Jamaican as being pan-Caribbean, the signature Jamaican dish ackee and saltfish can turn up on almost any island. Known by the scientific name *blighia sapida,* the fruit is bright red. When ripe, it bursts open to reveal three large black seeds and a bright yellow flesh that some say resembles scrambled eggs. This is what turns up with saltfish, or anything else in the Caribbean.

Allspice: In one of those linguistic ironies, the island that grows virtually all of the world's supply of allspice doesn't call it allspice at all. On Jamaica, it's

known as pimento (the tree from which allspice comes), thus opening the door for confusion with the same Spanish word for pepper and the popular product of roasted red bell peppers sold in water or oil. The spice got its "market name" away from Jamaica because it reminded tasters of cinnamon, nutmeg, mace, black pepper and clove, *all* together. Allspice finds its greatest popularity in English and Spanish colonies all over the world.

Avocado: The rallying cry of the avocado industry in recent years has become, "It Isn't Just for Guacamole Anymore!" Though the bright green Tex-Mex appetizer remains many people's introduction to avocado, the once-exotic fruit native to Mexico, Central America and parts of South America is turning up in other settings, too. Avocado is one of the truly ancient food traditions of the Americas, being enjoyed by Toltecs, Aztecs and Incas long before the European conquerors arrived. These conquerors took the avocado back to Europe and eventually expanded its cultivation to Hawaii, Africa and Polynesia.

Boniato: In Hispanic markets, this starch can turn up as batata, white yam or Cuban sweet potato, though we've also heard it described as camote, kumara or Florida yam. Its patch skin is reddish-pink, while its flesh is creamy and white. When cooked like sweet potatoes, boniato has a mild flavor that reminds some of chestnut. You also can find boniato sold as a sweetened paste called dulce de batata, or as boniatillos-boiled-down preserves lightly dusted with confectioners' sugar.

Breadfruit: This large green fruit made the voyage to Jamaica from its native Tahiti in 1793 ... yet another agriculture product brought to a different hemisphere by Captain Bligh. Breadfruit is notable for its pebbly green skin and potato-like texture inside, the latter explaining why it's used often when plain "Irish potatoes" are not available. In the Caribbean, we seen breadfruit chips, breadfruit fries and even breadfruit salad at picnics. Breadfruit is generally picked and eaten before it ripens. Typically treated like squash, it can be baked, grilled, fried, boiled or roasted after being stuffed with meat.

Calabaza: This is the name given most often to West Indian pumpkin, not to be confused with the bright orange vegetable carved in America for Halloween or used to make American pumpkin pie. A member of the gourd, squash and melon family, calabaza has a slightly sweet flavor similar to that of butternut squash. By virtue of a firm texture that stands up to long cooking, calabaza is often included to "stretch" the meat and other vegetables in soups and stews. It is also used throughout the tropics in breads and, with plenty of sugar, in dessert puddings.

Callaloo: A leafy, spinach-like vegetable, callaloo holds roughly the same place in Caribbean culture that greens like mustard, turnip or collard enjoy in the Deep South. It's been turning up spelled a dozen different ways in handwritten and home-printed island recipe books all the way back to 1696. Also known as Chinese spinach or Indian kale, the variety known officially as *Amaranthus viridis* should not be confused with the "callaloo" of the Eastern

Caribbean, which is a misnomer for the leaves of the dasheen plant.

Cho-Cho: In New Orleans, it's tough not to call these lovely green vegetables by the local French name, mirlitons. But they are affectionately known as cho-cho in much of the tropical world. Other names include chayote in most Hispanic cultures, christophene on some islands, and even the generic-sounding vegetable pear (they are shaped like pears, after all). Though most often eaten as a vegetable—stuffed, baked, sliced and lightly blanched to give crunch to salads—they are also considered an apple substitute on islands without apples. Cho-cho pie, for instance, is a favorite.

Coconut: Virtually no other ingredient on Earth speaks the word "tropical" with quite the eloquence of coconut. Whenever people think of the tropics, they think of the coconut palms swaying in the trade winds on a blindingly white beach ... or sipping a drink that includes coconut from the coconut shell itself. The coconut probably originated in southern Asia, particularly in Malaysia; but thanks to its buoyancy and waterproof shell, it has been able to float away to distant shores throughout the tropical world. Especially popular is the creamy "milk" produced by squeezing the grated white flesh.

Conch: For the longest time, Americans who sampled conch at all did so in the Florida Keys (in Key West, natives of the island proudly call themselves Conchs and their hometown the Conch Republic) or in the Bahamas. What they tasted was usually fritters with pieces of conch finely chopped and pounded, or a

tomato-based chowder that tenderized the conch much the same. With the tender baby conch from the Turks and Caicos, none of this treatment is required. That's why we're able to use it in more dishes with less disguises, such as simple conch ceviche.

Crabmeat: Most parts of the tropics have access to some form of crab. In New Orleans, it's a tradition surrounded by nostalgia's glow to boil blue crabs in seasoned water (these spice mixes are sold as "crab boil") and then pour the now-red crabs out on a table covered with newspaper. This is done in the Caribbean as well, with a slightly different blend of spices. In addition, the crabmeat picked from cooked crabs becomes a delicacy fraught with possibility. One popular and rustic way to serve crabmeat is mixed with breadcrumbs and seasoning and stuffed back into the cleaned shell. In the Caribbean, these are called Crab Backs.

Fleur de Sel: Salt, of course, is one of the world's oldest flavor enhancers and preservatives, giving it a value almost beyond price in many ancient cultures. In addition to serving as currency in primitive dealings, it was the stuff with which fortunes were made and over which battles were fought. Going back millennia, salt came not from shakers or canisters but from the sea, and from very early times, fleur de sel was considered the finest salt on Earth. This "flower of salt" is hand-harvested by workers who gently scrape up only the delicate top layer. Dominique's Fleur de Sel is harvested by these very methods on his native island of Mauritius.

Ginger: For thousands of years, gingerroot was used for flavor and health by the cultures of the Far East.

It made its way with the opening of trade from Asia to the Mediterranean and Europe, and from there was introduced by the Spaniards to their holdings in Latin America and the West Indies. Though still popularly held to be an "Asian" ingredient, figuring notably in Chinese, Thai and Vietnamese dishes (and in pickled form as part of Japanese sushi), ginger can add brightness and spice to almost any dish. People of the Caribbean islands also produce steeped teas and even beers flavored with ginger.

Goat: How the Caribbean came to eat goat—and especially came to consider it part of their cuisine—says everything about the traditions of the melting pot. When immigrants from India came to the islands in the 19th century, after the emancipation of the slaves, they gathered everything they needed to prepare their essential-to-life curries. But the islands had no lamb. A goat must have wandered by, and you can write the rest of the history. Goat is usually milder than lamb, to the surprise of first-timers. And, of course, if you can't find goat, you can substitute lamb right back again.

Guava: All over the tropical world, people love these small fruits with pink, seed-filled flesh. Though guavas are delicious when eaten raw, they most often find their personality expressed in jellies, preserves, fruit cups, sauces, cocktails and desserts. They are sweet when ripe but have a pleasant tartness when still green, which makes them perfect to add texture to salads, ceviche and the like. In ethnic markets, you'll find the fruit sold as guayaba in the general Latin world, guayaru in Haiti and goiaba in Brazil. Guavas have some of the nicest and most insistent perfume of any tropical fruit, and that's saying a noseful.

Jicama: When you're looking for cooling crunch, it's hard to beat jicama from Mexico, also known there as the Mexican potato and yam bean. The flesh has the mild, slightly sweet taste you'd probably expect looking at its pale color. For most people, jicama is more about texture than taste. Jicama can be part of so many cool dishes from the Mexican repertoire ... diced and tossed with cubed avocado, onion, lime juice, cilantro and salt, or tossed with green apple slices and tomatillos. In Mexico, jicama is combined with shredded coconut in the candy dulces de jicama and coco.

Lime: The popularity of this bright green citrus fruit spread throughout the world with the British Navy in the 18th century, especially after its physicians realized that regular consumption of the juice helped sailors avoid scurvy. It wasn't long before British seamen and finally all British people were known colloquially as "limeys." In the tropical world, limes (including the small, yellow Key limes used in Florida's famous Key lime pie) are one of the most important ingredients in sauces and marinades, and are used to perk up dishes ranging from savory to sweet. Chicken and fish especially benefit from a squeeze of fresh lime.

Lobster: In the United States, the "magic word" to describe most delectable lobsters is "Maine," for that Atlantic Coast state supplies much of what began as a New England food fetish and spread out from there. In many parts of the warm-weather world, however, it's the clawless spiny or Caribbean lobster that rules. People of the West Indies, in fact, share their appreciation of this seafood with their brethren in the Bahamas and Florida, where Maine lobsters seem a kind of affectation. The same creatures are devoured as the langouste of France, the aragosta of Italy and the langosta of Spain.

Lychee: This fruit comes to tropical cooking from a deep rooting in the history of Asia. China is the world's largest producer, having gotten pretty good at it after more than 2,000 years. Today, with the increasing market for lychee reaching out into non-Asian cuisines, there are smaller industries devoted to its cultivation in India, Thailand, Taiwan, South Africa, Australia, Hawaii, Mexico and south Florida. Lychee lovers prefer their fruit fresh and just slipped from its shell, but it often finds a happy home in desserts mixed with strawberry, mango and kiwi.

Malanga: Among the most popular of starches used in Latin cooking (as well as in its newer, more stylish edition, New Southwestern Cuisine), malanga sometimes goes by yautia, tannier, Tania and cocoyam. Sometimes it's even confused with its close relative called taro. The yellow tint in the skin of true malanga is a clue, inspiring some to call the real deal malanga amarilla. With its nutty-potato flavor and starchy flesh, malanga can be used in almost any potato recipe—boiled, fried, roasted or mashed.

Mango: Though there are several competitors for the title, a certain pride of places attaches itself to mango, the "fruit of the tropics." Surely part of this title was the fruit's early success being grown in south Florida, turning up on New World and so-called "Floribbean" menus for years. Green (unripe) mangoes are used in hot sauces, chutneys and other condiments, while the ripe versions are popular in desserts, sweet snacks and a variety of cocktails. Actually a native of India, mango turns up in quite a few varieties, including Bombay, East Indian, St. Julian and Hayden.

Nutmeg: People raised in the tropics love spice, and this is never to be confused with "heat"—a different taste sensation altogether. One of their favorite spices, for both sweet and savory dishes, is this highly fragrant nut from the fruit of a tropical evergreen. Known as nutmeg in English-speaking cultures, and nuez moscada to the Spanish, the freshly grated shavings on the interior lend a lightly floral aroma and a bittersweet flavor to meats and sausages along with preserves, custards and cakes. Nutmeg often is used in combination with cinnamon and mace, actually the net-like covering of nutmeg.

Papaya: Here is one of the most popular tropical fruits other than mango, but if you know it only as a sweet ripened fruit, you are missing a big part of its charm. Papaya is one of the few vegetables associated with South America that is actually native to there, though in the slave-influenced cultures of the Caribbean and Deep South, it is often known colloquially as "pawpaw." When ripe, the fruit has a bright orange color and a surprisingly bland flavor resembling squash. You'll see it often mixed with other tropical fruits. Green papaya is used in chutneys and other relishes in search of a crunch.

Passion Fruit: This fruit is enjoyed "with a passion" in cultures all over the tropical and subtropical worlds, including Hawaii, South America, Africa and New

Zealand. Yet to the disappointment of bartenders all over the islands, who say the name with a seductive wink, the reference is actually to the "passion" of Jesus within the Christian tradition. The parts of the lovely passion fruit flower remind some of the wounds, crucifixion nails, crown of thorns and apostles. Aside from its name, passion fruit is indeed a sensual delight, with intense aromas of citrus, honey and jasmine.

Peas: In many parts of the tropical world, "peas" is the affectionately generic name given to all pulses of legumes. Therefore, "peas" are not merely green peas or even black-eyed peas but kidney beans, navy beans and you-name-it beans. In cultures that have little money and therefore little access to meat, such peas or beans serve as a primary source of protein. Cooked with small pieces of salted pork or other affordable meat for flavor and seasoned with Scotch bonnet peppers, "rice and peas" (sometimes called the "national dish" of the Caribbean) becomes a nutritious meal. It also happens to be delicious.

Plantain: It may look like a banana, which is, of course a fruit, but a plantain should be treated as a vegetable. Some islanders actually call plantains "cooking bananas," a habit that only adds to the confusion. The fact is, plantains are larger and much starchier than bananas and never should be eaten raw. The ripe ones are especially good when fried and served as a tropical side dish. The bollos de platanos found in the Dominican Republic are fritters formed of mashed plantains and stuffed with cheese or meat, while the patacones of Colombia are flattened and deep-fried plantains used as a delivery system for meat, seafood or cheese.

Pork: Though Texas has worked to make the word "barbecue" synonymous with beef, pork has a stronger claim to history throughout the Caribbean islands. The wild hog was hunted by the now-extinct Arawak Indians, who preserved the meat by smoking it over low wood fires. Renegade sailors picked up the trick of smoking pork over these grills known as boucans, earning themselves a name in infamy as boucaniers (buccaneers, in English). Later, escaped African slaves known as Maroons perfected the process by covering the pork with a peppery herb paste. The Caribbean tradition of jerk pork was born, along with its distant non-island namesake "jerky."

Saltfish: In all the annals of colonial deprivation, few stories are as colorful and ironic as that of salted or smoked fish. Many parts of the New World had no access to fresh fish at all, so it became a habit of incoming Europeans to bring salt- or smoke-dried fish with them, ready to be rehydrated and enjoyed as the only fish available. Over the centuries, the taste of saltfish (also known as bacalao in Portugal and Brazil, or bacala in Italy) became so popular, even the arrival of fresh fish couldn't displace it. People from the tropics seek it out, wherever they find themselves.

Scotch Bonnet: On the world's Richter scale of hot peppers (actually known as the Scoville scale), the Scotch bonnet loved throughout the Caribbean is right at the top with its painfully kissin' kin, the habanero. The two peppers even look a lot alike—and taste a lot alike to those who dare to crunch down on them. These days, with the world's general fascination with spicy (meaning hot!) foods, Scotch bonnets and habaneros are available fresh, dried or ground, or processed into sauces with names like Jamaica Hell Fire. If you get your hands on a Scotch bonnet, be sure to wash them thoroughly afterward.

Sorrel: This unusual plant with origins in India was an early part of the English adventure in the New World, entering the Caribbean by way of Malaysia as far back as 1655. Part of its beloved status comes from its blooming in December, supplying deep red flowers for Christmas decorations on the English islands of Jamaica, Barbados and Antigua. Once its holiday duties are done, the flowers are dried and steeped in water to produce a bright red drink with a pleasantly tart flavor. Sorrel is also known as roselle and, most colorfully, as flor de Jamaica.

Star Fruit: There was a time when this was virtually the most exotic-looking fruit Americans encountered in the tropics, whether they heard it called carambola or by this highly visual name. As far as presentations are concerned, few things can look better than this fruit sliced crosswise to form a perfect star. Star fruit is a vital crop in many parts of Asia, South and Central America, the Caribbean and Hawaii, beginning its travels in Malaysia and passing into the trade routes by way of China. It was possibly first brought to the West by Chinese immigrants to Hawaii.

Tamarind: These brown pods from a decorative tree contain a sweet and tangy pulp that's used for flavoring everything from beverages to stews to sauces. That said, it should come as no surprise that tamarind pulp is part of the secret recipes for angostura bitters and Jamaica's famed Pickapeppa sauce. Tamarind is also an important part of Caribbean folk medicine. Whole tamarinds are sold in some supermarket produce departments or in West Indian, Hispanic or Asia groceries. Increasingly, commercial tamarind pulp or paste can be found in a jar.

Yam: In New Orleans and indeed all over the United States, there is confusion about the name of this starch. The product most often sold as "yams" in America may be a product known as "Louisiana yams," but they actually aren't yams at all. They're sweet potatoes. The misnomer supposedly goes back to language difficulties between English-speaking Southern plantation owners and their African slaves. In the tropics, true yams are tuberous roots more likely to be white than yellow or bright orange. They are wonderful treated like Irish potatoes, especially boiled or roasted.

Yucca: Known in the Caribbean as cassava, this starchy tuberous vegetable is most associated with Hispanic-American cuisines. Almost every meal in many Latin American cultures incorporates yucca in some form, from stews to dumplings to breads to puddings. In fact, yucca's most familiar form is in the dessert called tapioca. Africa also has a rich tradition of cooking with yucca, using the starch to thicken a rich stew of beef, tomato, onion and coconut milk in Kenya, and turning up with salted herring in Nigeria. Yucca, also spelled yuca, is native to Brazil.

Acknowledgments

Most of all, I would like to thank my teams at Dominique's and Bistro 38 by Dominique, starting with two of my partners—Pat Shimon, the Maison Dupuy's General Manager, and restaurant General Manager Walter Bertot. In the kitchen, this book and the many creations that satisfy our customers could not have been completed without the hard work of Executive Sous Chef Quan Tran and Sous Chef Levi Ealding, along with Maximiliano Iezzi, Mariano Fernandez, Juan Tarzia, Christian Sala, Mitch Dowling and Larry Butler.

I would also like to recognize our entire front-of-the-house service staff, which delivers our creations in a manner that completes our guests' experience.

In addition, I want to thank Chef Adrian Cordes and the entire team at our newest location, Bistro 38 by Dominique, at the newly opened New Orleans Marriott Metairie at Lakeway. They are already becoming part of our family that allows us to deliver great food, great wine and great service.

I would be remiss if I did not thank the partners that own the hotels housing the restaurants bearing my name—specifically, Morgan Stanley, Pyramid Hotel Group of Boston and their partners, who purchased both of these hotels just weeks before the catastrophe of Hurricane Katrina. With the help of Rick Kelleher, Warren Fields, Jim Dina, Bob Foley, Harry Greenblatt and Tico Bevier, we were able to take care of the associates at both hotels by providing temporary housing, ongoing employment opportunities and financial assistance. And through their commitment we were able to reopen these hotels, our two restaurants and, most importantly, participate in the rebirth of New Orleans.

For the foods used in testing these recipes and styling these lovely photographs, we were blessed with a true feeling of partnership from some of the best in the business: Dan Morgan at Morgan Ranch for the best American Kobe beef, Chuck Hesse at Turks and Caicos Conch Farm, and Stephen Garza at White Water Clams, along with our friends at Gary's Seafood, Inland Seafood, Buckhead Beef, Berkshire Pork, Capital Produce, Nando's Peri-Peri Sauce and Ultimate Spice Fleur de Sel.

At Bright Sky Press, considerable gratitude is due publisher Rue Judd, copy editor Kristine Krueger and book designer Isabel Lasater Hernandez.

Finally, I would like to offer my thanks and admiration to the people of New Orleans, who embraced me and my food from the start, for their perseverance and heroism in rebuilding our city. May the future shine bright for us all!

Recipe Index

A

Appetizers
Ahi Tuna and Crispy Pineapple, 22
Caribbean Conch Ceviche, 15
Cool Watercress-Romaine Salad, 31
Curried Lamb and Chickpea Samosas, 21
Foie Gras on Fried Plantain Rounds, 28
Grilled Lollipop Wings with Peri-Peri, 25
Haitian Conch Salad, 16
Meat Patties, 29
Peri-Peri Grilled Shrimp Caesar Salad, 30
Phyllo-Goat Cheese Purses with Onion
    Fricassee, 20
Pompano Tartare, 23
Salmon-Crabmeat Roses with Horseradish
    Crème Fraîche, 14
Shrimp and Foie Gras Ravioli with Leek
    Fondue, 27
Spicy Crawfish atop Fried Green Tomatoes, 19
Surf and Turf Ceviche, 17
Aromatic Basmati Rice, 104
Asian Pesto, 41

B

Bahian Lobster Moqueca, 69
Balinese Satay, 76
Banana Fritters with Coffee-Rum Sauce, 127
Beans
    Classic Rice and Peas, 105
    Conch and White Bean Chowder, 38
    Oxtail and Broad Beans, 97
    Oxtail and Pigeon Pea Soup, 42
    Red Bean Soup with Spinners, 45
Beef (also see Veal)
    Beef Pho with Ming's Asian Pesto, 41
    Braised Short Ribs, 90
    Gaucho Fillets, 89
    Island-Rubbed Steak, 91
    Meat Patties, 29
    Medallions with Rum-Butter Mushroom Sauce, 96
    Oxtail and Broad Beans, 97
    Stock, 148
    Surf and Turf Ceviche, 17

Ultimate Meat and Potatoes, 99
Beverages (see Drinks)
Blue Hawaii, 135
Boniato Galettes, 60
Braised Pork Belly and Breadfruit Escabèche, 86
Braised Short Ribs with Debris Cakes, 90
Breadfruit
    Chips, 83
    Escabèche, 86
    Soup with Truffles and Foie Gras, 43
Butternut Squash Debris Cakes, 90

C

Caipirinha,132
Cappamisu, 119
Caramelized Pineapple Tarte Tatin, 116
Ceviche
    Caribbean Conch, 15
    Surf and Turf, 17
Chicken
    Balinese Satay, 76
    Grilled Lollipop Wings, 25
    Mauritian Roti, 75
    Mulligatawny Soup, 36
    South African, 78
    Stock, 148
Chimichurri
    Cream Cheese, 89
    Lemon Mustard, 144
    Oven-Dried Tomato, 144
    Pork Chops with Pork Confit-Yucca Fritters, 84
    Roasted Tomatillo, 144
Chocolate
    Glazed Papaya Cake, 121
    Soufflés, 123
Chowder, Conch and White Bean, 38
Chutney
    Cashew Nut, 76
    Tamarind Coconut, 107
Clams, Red Stripe, 55
Classic Cuban Mojito, 133
Classic Rice and Peas, 105
Coconut Crab Soup, 37
Coconut Milk, 147

Conch
    and White Bean Chowder, 38
    Caribbean Ceviche, 15
    Haitian Salad, 16
    with Cho-Cho Risotto, 63
Cool Watercress-Romaine Salad, 31
Cornish Hens, Thyme-Roasted, 83
Couscous, Saffron Cakes, 103
Crab
    Coconut Soup, 37
    Salmon-Crabmeat Roses, 14
    Stock, 148
Cracked Conch with Cho-Cho Risotto, 63
Crawfish
    and Watercress Soup, 34
    atop Fried Green Tomatoes, 19
    Stock, 148
Creole Cobia, 59
Curry
    Curried Goat in a Bread Bowl, 79
    Curried Lamb and Chickpea Samosas, 21
    Homemade Powder, 140
    Lobster Rougail, 68
    Meat Patties, 29
    Mulligatawny Soup, 36
    Shrimp-Curry Essence, 59

D

Daiquiri
    Original, 135
    Passion Fruit, 132
Desserts
    Banana Fritters with Coffee-Rum Sauce, 127
    Cappamisu, 119
    Caramelized Pineapple Tarte Tatin, 116
    Chocolate-Glazed Papaya Cake, 121
    Chocolate Soufflés, 123
    Flambéed Pineapple, 129
    Floating Island with Crème Anglaise, 120
    Key Lime Crème Brûlée, 129
    Lemongrass Panna Cotta, 115
    Mango and Coconut Soufflé Glacé, 113
    Piña Colada Rice Pudding, 128
    West African Sweet Potato Pie, 124

Drinks
    Blue Hawaii, 135
    Caipirinha, 132
    Classic Cuban Mojito, 133
    Island Coffee, 137
    Island Sky, 133
    Mai Tai, 134
    Mango Margarita, 135
    Nonalcoholic Tropical Punch, 137
    Original Daiquiri, 135
    Passion Fruit Daiquiri, 132
    Piña Colada, 134
    Pink Lady, 134
    Planter's Punch, 136
    Reggae Sunsplash, 136
    Rum Collins, 136
    Yellow Bird, 132
Duck Stock, 148

F

Farata, 75
Fish (also see Snapper)
    Ahi Tuna and Crispy Pineapple, 22
    Creole Cobia, 59
    Pompano Tartare, 23
    Sweet-Hot Swordfish en Brochette, 67
Flambéed Pineapple, 129
Floating Island with Crème Anglaise, 120
Foie Gras
    Breadfruit Soup with Truffles and Foie Gras, 43
    on Fried Plantain Rounds, 28
    Shrimp and Foie Gras Ravioli, 27
Fried Green Tomatoes, 19
Fritters
    Banana, 127
    Pork-Confit Yucca, 84
    Spiced Lentil-White Corn, 81

G

Garam Masala, Homemade, 140
Garlic Mashed Potatoes, 102
Gaucho Beef Fillets, 89
Gazpacho with Creole Mustard Ice Cream, 49
Golden Potato Cakes, 102
Grapefruit and Scotch Bonnet Mojo, 145
Grilled Lollipop Wings with Peri-Peri, 25

H

Haitian Conch Salad, 16
Harissa, 144

Homemade Curry Powder, 140
Homemade Garam Masala, 140
Homemade Mayonnaise, 147
Horseradish Crème Fraîche, 14

I

Ice Cream
    Creole Mustard, 49
    Crystallized Ginger, 116
Indian Pickled Vegetables, 106
Indian Vindaye, 142
Island Coffee, 137
Island-Rubbed Steak, 91
Island Sky, 133

J

Jerk Marinade, 141
Jerk-Marinated Roast Leg of Lamb, 94
Jerk Pork Tenderloin, 95
Jicama-Grapefruit Slaw, 95

K

Key Lime Crème Brûlée, 129

L

Lamb
    Curried Lamb and Chickpea Samosas, 21
    Jerk-Marinated Roast Leg of Lamb, 94
    Meat Patties, 29
    Merquez Sausage, 93
    Rack of, 93
    Terrine, 93
Leek Fondue, 27
Lemons, Pickled, 143
Lemongrass Panna Cotta, 115
Lobster
    Bahian Moqueca, 69
    Rougail, 68
    Stock, 149
Louisiana Shrimp with Boniato Galettes, 60

M

Mai Tai, 134
Mango
    and Coconut Soufflé Glacé, 113
    Margarita, 135
    Pickled Green, 142
    Soup with Lime Zest, 44
Marinade, Jerk, 141
Mauritian Chicken Roti, 75

Mauritius Fleur de Sel Baked Snapper, 52
Mayonnaise, Homemade, 147
Meat Patties, 29
Merquez Sausage, 93
Mirlitons
    Au Gratin, 109
    Cho-Cho Risotto, 63
Mojito
    Classic Cuban, 133
    Grilled Scallops, 64
Mojo, Grapefruit and Scotch Bonnet, 145
Mulligatawny Soup, 36

N

Nasi Goreng, 76
Nonalcoholic Tropical Punch, 137

O

Original Daiquiri, 135
Oven-Dried Tomato Ratatouille, 103
Oven-Dried Tomatoes, 31
Oxtail
    and Broad Beans, 97
    and Pigeon Pea Soup, 42
Oysters
    Saffron Oyster Toasts, 34
    Surf and Turf Ceviche, 17

P

Passion Fruit Daiquiri, 132
Pepperpot, 47
Peri-Peri Grilled Shrimp Caesar Salad, 30
Peri-Peri Sauce, 141
Phyllo-Goat Cheese Purses with Onion Fricassee, 20
Pickled Green Mangoes, 142
Pickled Lemons, 143
Piña Colada, 134
Piña Colada Rice Pudding, 128
Pineapple Mille-Feuille, 22
Pink Lady, 134
Plantains, Fried Round, 28
Planter's Punch, 136
Pompano Tartare, 23
Pork
    Braised Pork Belly, 86
    Chimichurri Chops, 84
    Jerk Tenderloin, 95
    Pepperpot, 47
Potatoes, Garlic Mashed, 102

R

Ratatouille, Oven-Dried Tomato, 103
Ravioli, Shrimp and Foie Gras, 27
Red Bean Soup with Spinners, 45
Red Stripe Clams, 55
Reggae Sunsplash, 136
Rice
    Aromatic Basmati, 104
    Cho-Cho Risotto, 63
    Classic Rice and Peas, 105
    Nasi Goreng, 76
    Spiced Jasmine, 104
Roasted Tomatillo Chimichurri, 144
Rum Collins, 136

S

Saffron Couscous Cakes, 103
Salads
    Cool Watercress-Romaine, 31
    Haitian Conch, 16
    Peri-Peri Grilled Shrimp Caesar, 30
    Summertime Fish, 70
    Watercress, 90
Salmon-Crabmeat Roses with Horseradish Crème
    Fraîche, 14
Sauces
    Chimichurri, 144
    Harissa, 144
    Peri-Peri, 141
    Raita, 145
    Rum-Butter Mushroom, 96
Scallops, Mojito Grilled, 64
Seafood (see Clams, Conch, Crabmeat, Crawfish,
    Fish, Lobster, Oysters, Scallops, Snapper and
    Shrimp)
Shallot Jus, 89
Shrimp
    and Artichoke Soup, 35
    and Foie Gras Ravioli with Leek Fondue, 27
    and Okra Fricassee, 59
    Croquettes, 56
    Curry Essence, 59
    Louisiana, 60
    Peri-Peri Grilled, 30
    Skewers with Tamarind Butter, 65
    Stock, 149
Side Dishes
    Aromatic Basmati Rice, 104
    Boniato Galettes, 60

Breadfruit Chips, 83
Breadfruit Escabèche, 86
Butternut Squash Debris Cakes, 90
Cashew Nut Chutney, 76
Cho-Cho Risotto, 63
Classic Rice and Peas, 105
Garlic Mashed Potatoes, 102
Golden Potato Cakes, 102
Indian Pickled Vegetables, 106
Jicama-Grapefruit Slaw, 95
Mirlitons Au Gratin, 109
Nasi Goreng, 76
Oven-Dried Tomato Ratatouille, 103
Pork Confit-Yucca Fritters, 84
Saffron Couscous Cakes, 103
Shrimp and Okra Fricassee, 59
Smothered Callaloo, 86
Spiced Jasmine Rice, 104
Spiced Lentil-White Corn Fritters, 81
Tamarind Coconut Chutney, 107
Simple Syrup, 133
Snapper
    Mauritius Fleur de Sel Baked, 52
    Roasted Whole Red, 71
    Simple Seared, 57
    Smoked Rillette, 46
    Summertime Fish Salad, 70
    Yellowtail with Shrimp Croquettes, 56
Soups
    Beef Pho, 41
    Breadfruit, 43
    Coconut Crab, 37
    Crawfish and Watercress, 34
    Gazpacho, 49
    Mango, 44
    Mulligatawny, 36
    Oxtail and Pigeon Pea, 42
    Pepperpot, 47
    Red Bean, 45
    Shrimp and Artichoke, 35
    Surprise Coconut Shrimp, 46
South African Chicken, 78
Spiced Jasmine Rice, 104
Spices
    Homemade Curry Powder, 140
    Homemade Garam Masala, 140
Spicy Crawfish atop Fried Green Tomatoes, 19
Stock
    Beef, 148
    Chicken, 148

Crab, 148
Crawfish, 148
Duck, 148
Lobster, 149
Shrimp, 149
Veal, 148
Sugarcane-Skewered Sweetbreads, 81
Surf and Turf Ceviche, 17
Surprise Coconut Shrimp Soup, 46
Sweet-Hot Swordfish en Brochette, 67

T

Tamarind
    Butter, 65
    Coconut Chutney, 107
    Ginger Dressing, 15
    Purée, 146
Thyme-Roasted Cornish Hens with Breadfruit
    Chips, 83
Trio of Lamb, 93

U

Ultimate Meat and Potatoes, 99

V

Veal
    Stock, 148
    Sugarcane-Skewered Sweetbreads, 81
Vegetables, Indian Pickled, 106
Vinaigrettes
    Citrus-Mustard, 31
    Soy-Ginger, 22
Vindaye, Indian, 142

W

West African Sweet Potato Pie, 124

Y

Yellow Bird, 132
Yellowtail Snapper with Shrimp Croquettes, 56
Yucca
    Croutons, 42
    Pork Confit Fritters, 84